REAL
Women
IN
REAL ESTATE

Unleashing Her Power:
Inspiring Stories and Strategies

Quantity sales and special discounts are available on quantity purchases by corporations, associations, and others. For details, contact the publisher at the address above.

Orders by U.S. trade bookstores and wholesalers. Email info@BeyondPublishing.net

The Beyond Publishing Speakers Bureau can bring authors to your live event. For more information or to book an event contact the Beyond Publishing Speakers Bureau speak@BeyondPublishing.net

The Author can be reached directly at BeyondPublishing.net

Manufactured and printed in the United States of America distributed globally by BeyondPublishing.net

BEYOND
PUBLISHING

New York | Los Angeles | London | Sydney

ISBN Softcover: 978-1-63792-593-5
ISBN Hardcover: 978-1-63792-576-8

TABLE OF CONTENTS

FOREWORD

REAL WOMEN IN REAL ESTATE

Unleashing Her Power: Inspiring Stories and Strategies

Buckle your seatbelts, because we're about to embark on an exhilarating journey through the world of real estate investing! Welcome to "Real Women in Real Estate: Unleashing Her Power" – a book that will have you feeling like a superhero in no time. Get ready to don your investing cape and harness the power of bricks and mortar to build generational wealth!

As a real estate entrepreneur who has weathered the storms of this wild industry, I can assure you that there's more to investing than meets the eye. I've learned many lessons and poured countless amounts of blood, sweat, and tears into buying and selling over $1 Billion in multifamily assets. It's a realm where women, especially women of color, have often been relegated to the shadows – but guess what? We're about to shine brighter than a supernova, and this book is the perfect launchpad!

Picture this: a group of mighty women armed with knowledge, resilience, and an uncanny ability to spot a great deal from a mile away. We're not just breaking glass ceilings; we're bulldozing through them with a force that will make even the most seasoned investors take notice. And we are doing it in a fabulous pair of high heels!

In "Real Women in Real Estate," we're flipping the script, both literally and figuratively. Gone are the days when investing was considered a good old boys' club. It's time for us to crash the party, set up shop, and show the world that women are not just a vital part of the equation; we're the secret ingredient that takes success to new heights! The true alpha males of the real estate world already know this secret and have been championing us, and for that, we thank you. We have come a long way, but we still have a long way to go.

Diversity is not just a buzzword; it's our secret weapon, our superpower. Within the realm of real estate investing, diversity of perspectives, experiences, and backgrounds is the fuel that ignites innovation and propels us forward. When women of color unite, our collective strength becomes an unstoppable force that challenges the status quo and transforms the investment landscape. We understand that diversity is not just a checkbox to be ticked; it is the very fabric of our success.

Within these pages, you'll meet a cast of awe-inspiring women who have conquered challenges, scaled mountains of doubt, and turned setbacks into stepping stones. Their stories will have you laughing, crying, and fist-pumping with joy. But hold on tight because we're not stopping there. These brilliant women are also handing out gold nuggets of wisdom, sharing the strategies that have propelled them toward greatness– something I wish I had when I first started over a decade ago.

Now, investing in real estate isn't all rainbows and sunshine. We'll encounter a few speed bumps along the way, but fear not! Think of me as your trusty tour guide, navigating you through the labyrinth of real estate with a dash of humor and a sprinkle of puns. Together, we'll find those hidden gems, turn them into diamonds, and build a fortress of financial freedom!

Remember, ladies and gentlemen, the power of women in the investment space is not to be underestimated. We bring creativity, intuition, and a fresh perspective to the table. We're like real estate superheroes, swooping in to save the day, one profitable deal at a time. It's time to unleash the force within us and rewrite the narrative of investing, leaving a lasting legacy that will inspire generations to come.

So, buckle up and get ready for the adventure of a lifetime. "Real Women in Real Estate: Unleashing Her Power" is not just a book; it's a roller coaster ride through triumphs and trials, with laughter as our soundtrack and success as our destination. Let's embark on this

journey together and show the world what happens when women of color take charge and build their empires, brick by brick. You don't want to miss the gems hidden within these very pages, so what are you waiting for? Let's dive in!

Veena Jetti
Vive Funds

Chapter 1

THE SERENDIPITOUS
ENCOUNTER

Migena Agaraj

When I think back to the beginning of my journey into multifamily investing. I can't help but wonder if it was destiny or a chance encounter. After all, I was full of curiosity and ambition. But on the other hand, I really had no idea that I would end up at a multifamily event.

Multifamily Real Estate found its way into my life in 2021 when I least expected it. It started with casual conversations on Clubhouse, a social media app created during Covid. There I stumbled upon many captivating discussions about topics I was familiar with and many which I wasn't. Property investments, Multifamily, Limited Partnership, General Partnership, Cash Flow, etc. were new to me.

Intrigued, my interest grew, and with it, a yearning to explore this realm further.

Driven by curiosity, I began to attend more Clubhouse rooms, all things real estate. Sometimes there would be dozens of people attending, and oftentimes hundreds. I realized when certain clubhouse members would enter the virtual spaces, the number of participants would grow rapidly. Many were passionate about the different types of real estate. But when it came to multi-family, I had never heard anyone speak with more passionate determination than Grant Cardone.

I had no idea who he was. All I knew in 2021 was that every time he entered a clubhouse room, the numbers of club members would go up by hundreds, even thousands in minutes. My curious personality led me to start following Grant. Toward the end of the year, he was hosting a Real Estate Summit in Miami, and I decided that I had to attend. Of course, tickets were sold out when I wanted to buy one. I was determined to be at that event, no matter what. I only had to figure out how. Looking back, this lesson is Real: Decide, then figure out how later.

With determination fueling my decision, I sent a direct message to Grant on Clubhouse: "I missed the VIP Ticket. May I please have access to purchase one? Pretty Please…?"

I sent it and moved on with my day. What was the worst that could happen? He would not respond, and I would not attend the event in December. However, I knew I needed to try, even if it meant me asking the source directly.

It must have been fate because the universe heard me! Grant responded and shared an email address. I connected with Annie, his assistant, and on 12/12/2021, I flew to Miami for my first Multifamily event! Even though I was traveling alone, I didn't feel alone. I was accompanied by my drive, curiosity, strength, bravery, desire to learn, and many other emotions.

The RE Summit

My decision to attend the event proved to be a catalyst for growth. I soaked up knowledge, eagerly taking notes and absorbing every valuable insight shared on stage. The platform was interactive and helped me gain a deeper understanding of the nuances within the real estate landscape. The success stories were real, raw, and inspiring. I was wondering what had taken me so long to act. Why not sooner? Why now? How many years behind was I? None of these questions were helping me stay focused. I paused, reflected, and a beautiful feeling of freedom took over me. Why not now? Why sooner? How about *now*? How many years *ahead* was I? This was the room I was supposed to be in. These are the stories I was meant to hear and the people I was destined to meet. I was grateful to be there and was looking forward to the new journey. I decided then and there that there was no going back. I would commit to multifamily until I became successful.

The impact of the event extended beyond the educational aspect. Networking became a vital component of my experience, allowing me to connect with professionals from various sectors of the industry. Conversations flowed freely, and everyone I met was generous with their answers. This was where I met Brad, who became my mentor and partner. We both joined the Grant Cardone Real Estate Club at the 2021 Summit. The decision to join the real estate club marked a pivotal moment in our journeys—an opportunity to connect, learn, and grow alongside like-minded individuals who shared our passion for the real estate industry.

Many beautiful relationships were formed and promising partnerships were born. These connections opened doors to new opportunities, collaborations, and a support system of driven individuals who would become invaluable resources throughout my Real Estate Journey.

If earlier I felt it was my time to be introduced to this world, after the summit ended, I was convinced I was at the right time, meeting the right people who, as a collective, would contribute to my journey in RE.

From Action to Traction in the Unknown World of Multifamily

Leaving the event, I carried with me a renewed sense of purpose and a determination to translate the knowledge and inspiration gained, into action. My attitude shifted, thinking less about where life was taking me and more about where I was about to take life. The multifamily real estate event fueled my motivation, reaffirming my passion for a successful life and providing me with the tools, access, and proximity to the connections necessary to propel my journey forward.

There was potential for cash flow and long-term appreciation as well as the ability to make a positive impact on communities and have money work for us instead of the other way around. The element of surprise also provided me with a sense of adventure and excitement that fueled my progress. The anticipation of what each new day would bring, the thrill of uncharted territory, and the satisfaction of overcoming unexpected hurdles were constant reminders of the dynamic nature of the multifamily world. This fascination with the element of surprise kept me engaged, motivated, and eager to push the boundaries of what I thought was possible.

Then the impossible happened. I did not see this opportunity coming. It was just a few weeks after we joined the real estate club when Brad pitched a promising deal to the club. The presentation was captivating, and Grant immediately recognized both Brad and the potential of the deal.Intrigued by the opportunity, Grant asked Brad to connect with Annie, his assistant, to arrange a follow-up zoom call. Little did I know, Brad invited me to be on the call as well. I was nervous and excited at the same time. This was a beautiful gift from Brad. I was grateful, still am and always will be. That was a rare opportunity and I was not going to take it for granted.

I never anticipated such direct and unexpected involvement with a deal of this magnitude. I remember the excitement of the outcome of the upcoming call as if it happened yesterday. Little did I know that this unexpected opportunity would become a turning point in my multifamily journey.

The Zoom Call

The Zoom call served as a platform for exchanging ideas, sharing perspectives, and exploring the multifamily venture at hand. Grant's seasoned insights and strategic thinking complemented Brad's fresh perspective on the Multifamily and entrepreneurial spirit. Together, they formed a dynamic duo, inspiring me to think bigger, bolder, and more creatively about my multifamily journey. How did this happen? I could not believe my eyes. I was on a Zoom call with Grant Cardone and Brad. Was this meant to be, or was I an accidental participant?

The gift of trust extended by Brad in the form of the invitation to be a part of the unforeseen opportunity instilled in me a deep sense of responsibility. It became a driving force to show up fully, to bring my best self to the table, and to honor the belief placed in me. This was sacred. We both had invested time, money, and energy, yet none of us saw this opportunity coming. Brad and I have had many conversations about the Zoom with Grant. We always smile about the unique experience.

Grant sincerely wanted to help us and agreed to be a Key Principle (KP) on the deal Brad pitched. What did that mean? I was clueless and excited. I wanted to jump for joy without knowing why. I was under the influence of amazement. Game on. No more looking back. Are you curious to know how the deal went? I have a feeling many will reach out to find out if I don't share. . Many already know because they invested in that deal. I like to focus on the valuable lessons, the relationships built, and the smiles on people's faces – and my own – each time I tell the story. Fine, I'll share it :)

A month after our Zoom with Grant, Brad and I traveled to Aventura to attend "Bring your Deal Workshop." As we gathered, anticipation filled the air. The event was a culmination of Brad's efforts and my involvement at a level I had not even imagined let alone believe. A testament to the power of connection and collaboration within the real estate club. Brad was going to present the opportunity that captured not only the attention and excitement of the club members but of Grant himself. The presentation ignited a spark of inspiration, prompting us to think bigger and challenge our own beliefs about what was achievable. The energy in the room was electric as I absorbed the details of the opportunity, realizing the immense potential it held. The magnitude of what had transpired began to sink in. We realized that the seemingly impossible had become a reality. Raising millions in minutes was not just a distant fantasy; it had become our lived experience. That's right. We raised almost three million dollars in 20 minutes.

I could not keep up with the names and tried to memorize the faces of the club members who wanted to invest in the deal.

Show up!

In any journey, certain individuals have the power to ignite a spark, propelling us forward with unprecedented speed. Brad and Grant have been pivotal figures in my multifamily journey, emerging as KPs that accelerated the progress in ways I never imagined.

I have a question for you: Would the above have happened if I didn't show up in Miami? What if I went to the summit and did not take action to join the club? I doubt the Zoom with Grant and Brad would have taken place. What if Brad never invited me to participate on Zoom and be part of the deal? I believe we make things happen. I encourage you to begin to open the drawer of dreams, to wake them up, to give them life. Only then, will you fully live. There is a saying, "If you want your dreams to come true, wake up." Are you showing up for your dreams? Where? How? For whom? I recommend you start *now*. Get up, dress up, show up. The world needs to meet you. Decide now to meet yourself from a different angle and strike a pose in the process.

Storytelling

Dear reader, I bet you are wondering why I am sharing my journey with you. I'll probably never know your thoughts, or maybe I will, if we ever meet in person. Sharing our stories is a powerful act of service and responsibility. I hope to inspire others who may be on a similar path or contemplating their own journey real estate or something else. It doesn't matter.. Real estate can be a complex and challenging field. My intention is to ignite a spark of inspiration within the readers, encouraging them to pursue their dreams and overcome any obstacles they may encounter.

Reflection and Growth: Reflecting on our own experiences and sharing them with others can be a transformative process. As the author of my story, sharing it allows me to gain a deeper understanding of the lessons I've learned, the challenges I've faced, and the growth I've experienced. It also allows me to receive feedback, insights, and perspectives from readers, which can further enrich my own personal and professional development.

Leaving a Legacy: Sharing our stories is a way to leave a lasting impact and contribute to the collective knowledge and wisdom of future generations. By documenting my real estate journey, I hope to create a legacy that can inspire, guide, and inform others for centuries to come. It is my way of making a meaningful contribution to the real estate community and leaving a positive imprint.

In essence, I share my story with you, dear reader, because I believe in the power of storytelling to inspire, educate, connect, reflect, and leave a legacy. It is my hope that through sharing my experiences, I can make a meaningful difference in your real estate journey or the journey of your choice and contribute to the growth and success of others in this dynamic industry.

Still wondering what happened to the deal? We walked away from it. The numbers didn't make sense after the due diligence. Yet, this will always be my absolute favorite deal. It brought me amazing relationships based on trust. It taught me courage, determination. It also taught me not to lead with emotions. Protecting our investors is what matters most.

Ever since, I have not only invested in (as General Partner and Limited Partner) over 800+ units, but more importantly I have found a new passion! That passion is helping, educating, and working alongside all of my new colleagues and associates to start creating generational wealth, one relationship at a time!

Migena Agaraj

My name is Migena. I was born and raised in Albania in the beautful city of Fier. In 2003, I moved to York City, where I've lived ever since. I have worked as a hostess, cashier, waitress, captain in the restaurant, recruiter, supervisor, project manager, Area Director, and Director of Business Development (real estate). I am the CEO and founder of Eagles MA LLC, a consulting company for real estate services and beyond. I am a Global Focused Connector and Business Matchmaker, TV Host and Associate Producer of *America's Real Deal*, an investment TV show, and Bestselling author, inspirational speaker, 10X certified business coach, mentor, trainer, red carpet event host, and community builder. I am also a passive and active investor.

I love to travel. I speak five languages.

If I could eat one food forever, it would be honey.

I am active on all social media (LinkedIn, IG, Facebook, Twitter, Clubhouse, YouTube).

Check out my website: askmigena.com

Chapter 2

THE HONEY BADGER MENTALITY
IN REAL ESTATE

Fearless, Thick-Skinned, Resourceful, Unwavering, Ferocious

Brooke Ceballos-Pinero

"Ma'am, it was declined, and I've run it three times," said the Target employee at the cash register.

I looked at Macayla, who was five years old then, searching her face for answers. "What's taking so long, Mama? I have to pee!" she exclaimed, grabbing her crotch dramatically.

Marissa, two years old, angrily tried to remove the snap-on belt connected to her "cart cover" blanket for shopping carts. I looked back at the necessities already bagged in my cart, diapers, formula, tampons, Gerber graduate snacks, almond milk, crayons, a coloring book, and a bottle of wine 'cause life!

My face burned with embarrassment, and I felt my eyes filling with tears.

"How much does she owe? Said the woman behind me. "$89.21,"- the young boy at the cash register stated, looking even more uncomfortable than I was.

"Let me take care of you. I've been there. Just pay it forward when you're able." She was a middle-aged brunette woman with sparkling blue eyes. Today I would compare her to an older-looking Zooey

Deschanel. I hugged the woman who surprisingly hugged me back and got out of there with Macayla and Marissa with my ego crushed and happiness deflated, though I was grateful.

This was 2013 -10 years ago when I was in the middle of my divorce. I had always told myself I would never rely on a man for money. Now that my dual income was single, I realized I hadn't taken care of myself financially. Now I had to pay for rent, groceries, daycare, utilities, and ALL the things off $16.14 an hour plus commission working as a salesperson at the Petaluma, CA AT&T retail store.

Growing up, I had a scrappy childhood and spent most of it in survival mode. Without getting into the gory details, I had a single mom for most of my childhood, and she relied on the government, church, men, and friends to take care of us. She worked here and there, but I remember always moving and bouncing from house to house. I went to two different junior highs and three different high schools. I can't keep track of the grade schools. You can paint it as her being resourceful, a fighter, or whatever fits your scope, but growing up in that environment can paralyze or propel you.

Let's fast forward. Today is Sunday, 5/21/23, and I'm writing this from my couch in our living room with our Jack Russel-Dachshund Bella resting at my feet and my husband David playing video games to the left of me. I'm scratching my head, drinking my coffee, wondering how I will tell my story while inspiring others to act? From the beginning, that's how. ●

"I know you guys might see me as this guy that's great with sales and marketing but want to know where most of my financial success comes from? Real estate, apartment buildings to be exact."

I listened to Grant Cardone as he explained that with $3K in his pocket, he purchased 38 units as his first apartment building in San Diego, CA. This lit a cauldron of fire under my ass! In 18 months, I moved heaven and earth to make shit happen.

Let me catch you up. After reading Grant's 10X Rule, he said, "Don't be a little bitch" to all the Negative Nancy's, crybabies, and those that play the victims! Oh, I love this guy, I thought as I was on the freeway heading home after having my eyebrows micro-bladed. (Do it, ladies; it's fab! I recommend Morgan Finley in Santa Rosa, CA. Find her at FacesByMorgan on Instagram)

I started stalking him on social media and saw he offered a one-year mentorship to help accelerate sales. It was March 2020, and the world was on lockdown, so I needed creative ways to get customers' attention to grow sales for my day job. Working from home meant no in-person interactions, feet on the street, shaking hands, or kissing babies at events.

How in the hell was I supposed to sell fiber installations for buildings where nobody worked?

I had signed up for Grant's Sales and Marketing mentorship program to strategize with him during COVID, and when it was over, he gave me a VIP ticket to his first-ever Real Estate Summit and told me just to show up.

When I attended in July 2021, I was excited as I listened to Grant speak and elated by all the phenomenal people there and Grant's contagious energy. He had an offering for a 12-month Real Estate Club for "serious investors." Was I a serious investor? The only thing I invested in was my 401K, which was more annoying than a rollercoaster that you can't get off. However, I knew from my 18 years of hard time in the corporate world that I always wanted to open my own business, but what?

Jarrod Glandt, the President of Cardone Enterprises, got on stage, reminded us to act, and iterated that the time was now. My gut told me, **"If you don't do this, you will regret it."**

"Raise your hand if you're taking advantage of this opportunity?" Jarrod yelled out to the crowd on his microphone. "It's $25K to start the rest of your life!" Or something along those lines. What did they think we were? Billionaires like Grant? Luckily, I had left AT&T and had thousands of dollars in my bank account to roll over from my old 401K into my new 401k. That didn't happen. I was sold on investing in apartment buildings (multifamily) and was ALL in.

<u>I raised my hand, knowing that all Grant's salespeople were watching like hawks.</u>

Anthony Sisson, one of Grant's best sales guys, strolled over to me with a big grin. "What questions do you have regarding the Real Estate Club?" I responded, "Let's get this done. I'm hungry. Lunch is being served!"

Yes, I was one of the original gangstas in this now **immense** group. The only thing I had ever done in Real Estate was I bought my first home in July 2019. I had zero experience in any RE sector whatsoever. Stop saying you don't have experience or a real estate license. <u>Neither did I.</u> Stop coming up with reasons why you shouldn't do something that can change your life and start with reasons why you should.

The following 12 months after that were blood, sweat, tears, relentless daily action, and unforgettable experiences of touring properties while tackling best and finals. The highlight was Grant and I both being in best and final for The Hayworth. The shit-talking that our club witnessed during that friendly competition was fun! Neither one of us got that property, by the way. Even though there was much shit-talking between Grant and me, he has a big heart and truly wants to help people. I remember being at the Real Estate Summit, and with thousands watching, he threw me his jacket, which I immediately put on even though it made me sweat my ass off, I looked good in it, and it was Grant's! Thanks, Uncle G! That, my friends, is the power of SHOWING UP! Get off your ass and put yourself out there! "If they don't know you, they can't flow you!" -Grant Cardone.

On October 15, 2021, Empower Capital LLC was born, and I have never looked back. I have been building the Ceballos-Pinero empire and legacy to motivate women and marginalized communities to take advantage of their future daily, all while helping run my husband David's business, Sea Life Aquatics, which started from our passive income. TWENTY-ONE MONTHS later, by the way. We also have a blended family of four daughters Macayla, Marissa, Jaelynn & Laila ages 11-18 years old, working for a demanding W2 corporate job in Enterprise SaaS Sales in Global Trade, participating in podcasts, events, etc. Don't say you don't have time. You prioritize what's important. Stop Netflixin and chillin and grab your life by the horns! Nobody will hand you anything, nor are you entitled to anything you didn't work hard for.

BE YOU

Have you ever felt unseen, unheard, or forced to conform? Feel like you're always in survival mode? You're too loud, cover your tattoos, you're fat, you're skinny, you should straighten your hair, stop cussing, dress more feminine, you're so aggressive. Or my favorite: "Want to make a difference Brooke? Go work for a startup! #CorporateLife

Listen, our four daughters are women of color. I want them to see that nothing can stop them when they lead with love, have a servant mentality, and are unapologetically ambitious in their mission with consistent action and an inspiring community. What are your dreams? Goals? Aspirations? What could you do daily and never tire of? Create passive income with multifamily and GET AFTER IT.

What does investing in commercial real estate get you? **FREEDOM**

FREEDOM to spend your time how you like and with whom you want.

FREEDOM to travel. The world is the best teacher.

FREEDOM to give back on a massive level.

FREEDOM to fight injustices.

FREEDOM to be financially free and not owe anyone anything.

FREEDOM to be authentically you

Lead with God, health, family, community, wealth, and philanthropy.

9.88% of all women-owned businesses generate less than $100,000 yearly, and only 4.2% generate more than $1 million annually. (1a) Invest your money in real estate, get tax-free returns, and use that money to scale your business. Make your money work for you, not the other way around.

When I "make it," it will mean I can build La Escuela de Ceballos-Pinero in Guatemala for Nina Sofia, the beautiful young girl I've been sponsoring for two years who's a July baby like me and looks like my own children. Did you know they only get up to a 7th grade education there? La Escuela de Ceballos-Pinero will be from grades 8-12th.

When I "make it," it will mean I can take our family of six to Greece for a month to engulf ourselves in the blues and whites, enjoying my sacrifices and hard work. I told you, girls, that all my travel and days away would pay off. Mama kept her promise.

When I "make it," it will mean I'll be able to take our family and friends to travel with us privately, so we're not dealing with TSA, annoying gate changes, and flight delays. We'll walk to our private flight with drinks in our hands. VAMOS!

When I "make it," it will mean that when I see injustices happening, I'll have the money to support the policies to shut them down.

What are YOU going to do when you make it? Be the honey badger in this journey—fearless, thick-skinned, resourceful, unwavering, and ferocious. YOUR FUTURE SELF IS WAITING.

Collaborate with Brooke by scanning the below QR barcode. No camera? Find her on Instagram at brooklynn0719 or join her Facebook group at Our Seat At The Table. In this group, women and marginalized communities collaborate to gain financial freedom via multifamily and NNN investing.

1a: Online: Legal Jobs, Women Entrepreneurs Statistics, 5/20/23

Brooke Ceballos-Pinero

Brooke Ceballos-Pinero started as an LP investor acquiring 676 units and is a GP in 481 units and counting. She's using her 22 years of servant leadership experience in corporate America and her educational and team-sports background to build her active real estate portfolio. Brooke is part of the Grant Cardone RE Club, The Michael Blank Dealmaker Mastermind, Bay Area Investors, InvestHER, Sumrok's Millionaire Multifamily Mastermind, and more. She also interviews those who have closed their first deal on YouTube for Michael Blank. Brooke is the CEO of Empower Capital, where she empowers people financially, where they live, work, and play through investing. She is passionate about health and fitness, travel, women's empowerment, and providing a clear path to marginalized people to provide generational wealth while being a financial fiduciary. She enjoys baking with her daughters, Macayla and Marissa, dancing salsa, and hitting every food spot with her husband, David, in Northern California.

Chapter 3

RAISING MYSELF AND RAISING THE BAR

Letitia Montelongo

Latchkey to Financially Free

My brother and I were the poster children for the term "latchkey kids" in the '70's. Our parents struggled to make ends meet, so they always worked two or three jobs, and we, like many other kids growing up at that time, just never saw them. We raised ourselves. We moved a lot when we were kids so my dad could find work.

In April of 1978 my father came home and packed up his things, gave me a big hug, told me he loved me and then walked out the door. He had met another woman and was ready to start another life with her. He was my rock and I was heartbroken. He had taken all he could of the bills, the failed businesses, moving around the country looking for work and trying to raise two kids. My mom sat at the kitchen table crying while talking on the phone with my aunt. My family as I knew it, would never be the same.

My parent's were each other's third marriages, so stability was not something that ran in our family. My mom had decided she was going to move to live with my Aunt while she looked for another job.

Two months later, I decided that I needed to start taking care of myself so I went to Mexico with my boyfriend and at sixteen years old I got married. I finished my junior and senior year of high school as a married teenager and worked at nights to pay my bills. This is where I learned that nobody is going to do life for you, but YOU!

A few years later I started my own family. I had the desire to build a life where I could provide for my kids, but also spend quality time with them. I was a young mom of two beautiful girls. I worked hard and made my way into corporate America, landing a job in the marketing department at Sallie Mae. The first year, I was named Salesperson of the Year, and within a short time, I became the Senior Vice President of Sales and Marketing. Having a job with a Fortune 500 company was a dream come true. I thought I had really made it. I had a great salary, an expense account, and I was able to travel a lot with my girls. I was living the high life, and as a busy mom who had worked hard to get where I was, I felt like I was finally earning my due.

No Harvard Degree for Me

I never quite felt like myself surrounded by colleagues with Harvard degrees. I went to college one semester, but I already had two kids and I could never justify the amount of money I would make compared to the six years of my kids lives I would miss while going to night school, so I decided to just work harder. There's nothing wrong with an Ivy League education; that's great if you can do that, but I went the mom route, and there weren't enough hours in the day. I worked my way up the ladder instead of taking the elevator to the top.

Maybe this way, it made it easier for me to jump into the amazing world of entrepreneurship after the corporate downsizing of our company in 2008, along with the rest of America. I'd soon learn that having a degree, even from an Ivy League school, is not always a safety net, and many times, it might be the thing holding someone back from making the best decision of their lives.

The Road to Success Was Long and Hard and Filled with Potholes

In life, I don't think we always know where we'll end up; we just take what is the best option at the time, and after a series of right moves, we end up where we are. Hopefully, it's better than where we started. In 2008-2009, our management team had to lay off over a hundred people during the financial crisis and bank meltdown. I knew I was just biding my time, and I'd be next on the chopping block in short order.

They offered me a package to stay, but it meant cutting my salary by $100,000. Rather than stay and take the pay cut and watch the life get sucked out of me, I decided to take my severance and take the leap of faith unto the unknown.

Multiple Business Startups

Always the adventurous type with a marketing mind and an eye for opportunity, I felt like I had a three-month "safety net" and needed to figure things out quickly.

As a passionate person, I liked trying things, including starting businesses, seeing how far I could take them, and then selling them, re-tooling them, or spinning them off into something else.

Opening the first self-serve frozen yogurt shop on the south side of San Antonio, which became very successful, made me feel accomplished and proud. A few months into the business, we converted a food truck to sell frozen yogurt to our customers. Business was booming, especially on the weekends, with live music and families and people coming from everywhere – people loved us and were talking about us. During this time, I was part of helping start the San Antonio Food Truck Association. I would eventually sell that business to Orange Leaf, a national frozen yogurt chain. I went on to open a Med Spa, a small women's boutique that I opened with my daughter, a marketing company, and a medical device company in addition to launching a weekly financial show on Fox in San Antonio. Out of all this I was selected to be included in a book honoring the 50 most inspiring women in San Antonio.

Even though I'd had my real estate license since 2014 and believed that real estate was a good long-term investment, I never envisioned it creating substantial wealth for myself. I was not a novice in real estate; I just never considered multifamily real estate as a primary vehicle in my portfolio. I thought you had to be extremely wealthy to do that.

Local TV Host

Being a TV host and executive director of the show did have its advantages. I was already well-known in San Antonio events and networking. It was nice when I went out in public people recognized me. People gave me tickets to concerts, shows, and promos or VIP invites to restaurants and events. But one day, I got a call from a guy named Paul Montelongo, who said he'd been following my social media online and would like to interview me on his podcast. I knew of him and must say I was impressed with his business acumen, so I was excited to be on his podcast to talk about real estate.

Podcast to Proposal

It was an exceptionally fun interview, and I think both of us knew after a few dates on the other side of that podcast that there was more of a spark between us than just business. We had both been divorced for exactly 13 years. He had two sons; I had two daughters. We both loved the entrepreneurial life and could never work another J-O-B for someone else again! So not long after that first podcast, we tied the knot, and the rest is history!

Pandemic Boom Time

The pandemic was a tough time for a lot of people, and it was for us, too, for a bit. We were newlyweds with four kids, blending a family and navigating our new lives together when Covid hit in March of 2020. Even though our children were grown, we have a close nit family. My grandson was born a week before Covid, and we literally couldn't see him for two years. We were trying to figure out our lives and praying that God would take care of our children and grandchildren during that uncertain time. Making matters worse, realtors couldn't show houses. We had to figure out how to pivot. Paul had already been educating his inner circle for a good while on the finer points of real estate investing, so he began hosting weekly online Zoom educational webinars.

2.5 million in 16 months!

I'm a lifetime learner. I've always been into personal development and self-improvement and have always been looking for a better way to get things done. So, when Paul was teaching his real estate webinar during Covid, I jumped on the computer downstairs. I wanted to learn something, so I did. I learned how to underwrite deals. I took notes on every word my husband said. That 90-minute webinar, taught by Paul, soon brought us 2.5 million from just one deal. We went out and closed on a 64-unit property I found the very next week for $5 million. We'd turn around and sell it for 7.5 million 16 short months later! Our investors were so happy with us that they all stayed with us and reinvested in our next apartment acquisition.

Cancer Free

"Your test came back, and you have breast cancer," said my doctor of many years when Paul and I were in Las Vegas in 2020 at a Peak Partnership real estate conference. That phone call was at noon on that Saturday . We went to our hotel room and Paul and I hugged and cried and then WE decided that we were still going to beat this and we were still going to follow our goals and become an apartment power couple. I came home and went through surgery and radiation. During that time, we bought four apartment complexes. Thank God I'm in remission. Having each other and turning to our faith is what made the difference. Paul and I have both been students of and advocates for personal development our entire lives, which is one reason we are such a powerful match. That and our faith have helped us endure some challenging obstacles.

Speaking and Coaching

I love speaking. I love speaking to women's groups, real estate groups, investor groups, and at startup events not to mention online around the globe. Sharing on panels and being interviewed I come back to my core topics: personal freedom, time freedom, marketing, family, faith, and real estate.

Invest in Yourself

When I talk about investing in yourself, I am talking about improving your thoughts by feeding on positivity and personal development, but I'm also talking about investing in real estate. Real estate, in my opinion, is the safest long-term vehicle to create real wealth.

At Montelongo Capital, Paul and I have a close connection with our investors. We really want to get to know our partners and learn what drives them and makes them tick. We do an initial consultation to get to know potential investors to see if it is a fit. We won't take someone's money if we don't feel like it is a good fit. Once someone is on our team, it's all about communication, education, and training. We have weekly calls to educate and communicate with our investors and let them know what's going on with current and upcoming projects.

The most important thing Paul and I have learned together is to start big sooner. We both feel, individually and together, if we could go back and change anything, we both would have started bigger and sooner. Many times, it takes just as much work to close a multi-million-dollar multifamily deal as it does to close on a single piece of residential real estate. It just makes sense to put your journey to financial freedom on the fast track rather than taking the scenic route all day long!

Not to mention, when you're working with a team on vetted projects your risk is mitigated. There's always some risk, but when you have a team of experts that is hand-picking the best projects for you, you don't have to lose sleep wondering if you're getting the best bang for your buck.

We just landed a $42 million complex this month, which is our largest project to date. At Montelongo Capital, we are just getting started, and the best part is, there might be a place for you. We have many upcoming opportunities and would like to interview you to see if you're a fit with our family. Jump on our calendar today, and let's talk at MontelongoCapital.com.

Letitia Montelongo

"I had the pleasure of investing with Letitia, a dynamic lady with a big vision for herself and anyone who joins in with her on the journey of abundance. I feel blessed to know and invest with someone so driven, professional, and caring. Letitia is generous, kind, and patient in all her business practices.

The experience was a success! Not only did I receive my initial investment back, but the returns I made were beyond my expectations. Letitia and her husband, Paul, demonstrated their expertise and professionalism throughout the entire process, ensuring that every aspect of the investment was handled with care.

Their knowledge of the real estate market and their ability to identify lucrative opportunities impressed me. Thanks to their insights and guidance, I not only achieved excellent financial results but also gained valuable knowledge about real estate investing.

I highly recommend Letitia at Montelongo Capital to anyone looking for a trustworthy and successful investment partner in the real estate industry." ~ Peter Silvester

Letitia Montelongo, the co-founder and managing member of Montelongo Capital, is a powerhouse in the real estate industry. Not only does she excel in nurturing investor relationships and securing capital for multifamily property acquisitions, but she also possesses a fervent passion for teaching and coaching investors to scale their financial success to the next level.

With her real estate license dating back to 2014, Letitia has been instrumental in assisting buyers and investors in acquiring a diverse range of properties, including homes, warehouses, industrial sites, self-storage facilities, and multifamily properties. Her expertise lies in identifying undervalued and undermanaged multifamily properties, leveraging her skills to create exceptional opportunities for high returns in the commercial real estate sector.

Prior to immersing herself in the real estate realm, Letitia made significant contributions in higher education finance as a Senior Vice President for a Fortune 500 Company. However, in 2008, driven by an entrepreneurial spirit, she embarked on her own path, successfully owning and operating several small businesses such as Peachwave Self-Serve Frozen Yogurt, Yours Truly LA, Grace Advanced Aesthetics,

Lone Star Innovative Medical Solutions, and Letitia Montelongo Real Estate.

Today, Letitia and her husband Paul, channel their expertise and knowledge toward empowering others to achieve passive real estate investments, enabling them to unlock the freedom to live the life of their dreams. Alongside their four children and seven grandchildren, they proudly call San Antonio, Texas, their home.

Letitia Montelongo's exceptional skills in investor relations and capital acquisition and her dedication to teaching and coaching aspiring investors make her an influential figure in the real estate community. Her commitment to helping others scale their financial success to new heights is truly remarkable. With an outstanding track record in real estate, Letitia continues to leave an indelible impact on the industry through her expertise and passion for coaching others.

Chapter 4

FROM DESSERTS TO MULTIFAMILY:
A Journey to Financial Freedom

Jacqueline Landry

Pandemic Flashback – Told Partially in Third Person

Let's dive into the inspiring story of Jacqueline Landry, a determined wife working 80-plus hours a week running a dessert franchise striving to achieve the American Dream. Her journey serves as a testament of the many roadblocks and speed bumps that must be overcome in achieving one's dreams in multifamily real estate or any other business.

Jacqueline and her husband Melvin weren't always optimistic about their future but the harder they worked and the more they dove into personal development the clearer it became to them that multifamily real estate would be the long-term vehicle, the crown jewel of their retirement. Melvin had been working hard as a procurement supply chain professional, teaching college courses, and a landlord managing 50+ single-family homes in Pittsburgh. He and Jacqueline also had a new son, who was just 11 months old when Jacqueline started the dessert franchise.

Despite her hard work, Jacqueline found herself overwhelmed, trapped in a cycle of long hours and limited financial growth. Being parents, there just weren't enough hours in the day. Jacqueline and Melvin were both stressed beyond their limits with the franchise, seeing each other coming and going, lack of sleep, stress from responsibilities, and mounting bills. Not only had Jacqueline missed their son's first steps, at times, she would fall asleep at the wheel while driving home from work. This was a wakeup call for both her and Melvin – thank God that didn't end in disaster.

The exhaustion of working such long hours for four years and never receiving a paycheck inspired Jacqueline to seek a change that would offer her both time freedom and financial abundance. She made it a goal and a dream for them both to set themselves on a path to financial freedom through multifamily real estate. With Melvin's support and encouragement, Jacqueline began to believe now was the time, to take the baby steps toward their dream, and yes, they could indeed make it work if they just got started.

Melvin recounts, "After four years and losing over $1 million in the franchise, we decided to throw in the towel and close it. Then we were faced with the consequences of six-figure ligation bills, COVID, and online schooling for our little guy! What a year! "How in the hell are we going to get through this?"

My Husband Melvin is My Rock

My husband has been doing real estate since 2005 and in September 2022 is when my husband approached me and asked will I quit my job and join him in multifamily. My answer was "yes" and my last day in corporate America was October 28, 2022. Our mutual support for one another allows us to be an unstoppable team, and we are just getting started!

"In 2022 we found a multifamily ecosystem and coach. The lightbulb went on for us that this was the way to build wealth – with speed, while allowing us to spend time on what matters to us, which is building extraordinary memories with our friends and family (and not missing out on pivotable moments). We believe in the motto that education is the great equalizer, so we invested over $100,000 in multifamily educational and coaching programs."

Mindset Not Just Knowledge

At the beginning of my multifamily real estate journey, I joined my first Mastermind event. It was a combination camping and hotel trip. We primarily participated in the camping trip portion, as we had to return home early. The camping trip was focused on mindset. Within 30 minutes of arriving at the campsite, we learned about the benefits of hot (sauna) and cold (ice bath). When they instructed everyone to go to their tents and change into their bathing suit for these activities. I said to myself, "Holy crap, no way am I going to be able to do this." I didn't want to get in front of a camera or anyone else with my bathing suit on, let alone sit in an ice bath for two minutes or more.

Overcoming Fear

When I got in the line, I said to myself, "If these people can do it, why can't I do it?" There was no reason to believe that my body couldn't handle it if everyone else's could. Therefore, I changed my thought to" You know what, I'm going to do this," and I went all in. I had a coach with me that was encouraging and helping me through the first 30 seconds, which are the hardest. After that, I was good,

30 seconds in, I probably could have stayed for three minutes. When I got out, I was so proud of myself for doing it. That was a pivotal point for me. The people that around me were similarly minded, very supportive, and there was no way I going to let that group down or be an outsider. They really lifted me up and supported me through that challenge.

The rest of the trip consisted of mindset challenges such as walking for two hours in uneven terrain. I was able to do that as well. I also did yoga for the first time. During these challenges, it was amazing to see that when people wanted to give up, the group uplifted them and helped them keep going. Whether it was me or someone else in the group, there were constant words of support: "No, you better not quit, we're here, we're here to support you. You can make it to the top; you can make it through the two hours of running or walking." It was inspiring to be around so many like-minded people. I learned that many of these people were less fortunate than I was or had stories that were even more traumatic, but they had overcome their struggles and accomplished their goals. Many of them were well on their way to achieving financial freedom and forming a better life with less stress.

Maintaining Focus

Don't let your mindset distract you from achieving your lifelong goals. We've spent our time educating our friends and family with the hope that one day they too will understand the huge benefits of investing in multifamily, and we've had a few people come around, so we will keep planting seeds.

The thing that sets us apart as real estate investors is that we are realists. We tell it how it is. We don't try to sugarcoat stuff, as you can tell from our story. We know what heartache is and we know the amount of work it takes to run a franchise or be an active investor. We are here to educate and be real with our investors. There's a lot of hard work, and there are trials and tribulations, as with everything else you must go through in life. However, my husband and I work together as a support system to help our investors tackle their challenges and realize their goals.

We're Looking for 50-200 Doors

As we continue to delve further into multifamily real estate investing, we are looking to buy multiple smaller multifamily apartments in western Pennsylvania to increase our cash flow. These properties will be a buy and hold. We will also focus on long-term multifamily real estate investments in the Midwest, which means that there will be a 3 to 6-year hold before the property will be sold.

Months of Cash in the Bank - Pennsylvania and Beyond

Venturing into multifamily is not without risk; Melvin and I feel the best hedge to mitigate risk is to have a nice three-year cash cushion in the bank until we start getting those payout distributions on our 3–6-year investments. It's like starting a business. If you start a traditional business, you don't expect to break even until about year five, and that is if you're lucky and work hard. Do your due diligence, seek wise counsel, associate yourself with like-minded individuals who are doing what you aspire to do, and then jump in with both feet once you have your bases covered. Our long-term goal is financial freedom and generational wealth. I'm excited to see where we'll be in year four and beyond.

11 Investments in 12 Months

Imagine you've read all the books on training a horse, and you jump on its back and get thrown off. That can be dangerous and send you to the hospital. When the horse trainer arrives, he calmly mounts the horse and, in a few minutes, with a little instruction, the horse is behaving and obeying commands like it's been working with the trainer for years. That's what it looks like when you try to get into multifamily on your own by reading books at the library. Connecting with a mentor, joining an ecosystem, and collaborating to find a team that are, savvy, humble, educated, and proven real estate investors who have millions if not billions under management makes all the difference. We feel good about the 11 apartment buildings we are invested in. Being invested with that many apartment buildings that helps spread out the risk. If something goes south on one, two, or even three properties, we have the other properties to carry us through.

So, number one is to make sure your mindset is in place and number two is to make sure your finances are where they need to be to support your living expenses. Once that is lined up, you can begin educating yourself and building a supportive team around you to start your multifamily journey.

Inspiring Others to Join the Journey

Having achieved financial success and a life we love; we are passionate about helping others embark on their own paths toward passive residual income through multifamily. One the most common questions I get is, "Jackie, can you help me accelerate my wealth through apartment investing?" The answer is **YES**! We offer practical advice and encouragement for aspiring real estate investors, sharing strategies to overcome obstacles, mitigate risks, and find success in the industry. You can find more information and schedule a financial freedom call to discuss your situation in more detail by visiting our website www.morelandequity.com. You can also listen to our podcast on Spotify, YouTube, and Apple Podcast, "Get Diversified," for education and advice on different multifamily topics.

Our transformation from exhausted dessert franchise owners to thriving multifamily real estate investors showcases the power of seizing opportunities, embracing change, and taking calculated risks. Our story serves as an inspiration for individuals seeking financial freedom and a fulfilling life. By sharing our experiences, insights, and strategies, we encourage others to embark on their own journey towards passive income in the safe and lucrative world of multifamily real estate.

Jacqueline Landry

Jacqueline Landry is a certified project and change management professional, a licensed real estate agent in Pennsylvania and has over 17 years of experience in business consulting across multiple industries. Jacqueline graduated from the University of Illinois at Chicago with a bachelor's degree in accountancy. While going to school and after graduating, she worked for Arthur Andersen (one of the top 4 public accounting firms in the world). She dedicated 10 years to Arthur Andersen in various roles ranging from human resource clerk to manager in the business consulting division. After the demise of Arthur Andersen in 2002, Jacqueline worked for Federal Home Loan Bank of Chicago, West Monroe Partners, and others in a consulting capacity. In 2014, Jacqueline left corporate America to pursue her dreams of being a business owner. She ran and operated a franchise from 2015 and for many reasons decided to close the business in 2019. Jacqueline re-joined corporate America, working as a senior customer success manager for OneStream Software. She helped multi-million-dollar companies with getting them onboarded, overseen the implementation of the software, as well as assisted with complex issues. In Oct 2022, Jacqueline, and her husband Melvin Landry, decided that Jacqueline should leave her corporate job again and join her husband in the multifamily real estate business. Jacqueline and Melvin formed a company named More-Land Equity Capital. As of June 2023, Jacqueline and Melvin invested in 9 passive multifamily deals and are active partners in two deals.

You can find more about Jacqueline Landry by visiting our website *www.morelandequity.com* and you can jump on our calendar by scanning our QR code, can't wait to meet you!

Chapter 5

BUILDING YOUR HOUSE ON THE ROCK – A SOLID FOUNDATION

Faith, Family, Finances

Dezette Weathers

And the rain fell, and the floods came, and the winds blew and beat on that house, but it did not fall, because it had been founded on the rock. Matt 7:25

My parents embodied faith, love and resilience. They wanted the best for their nine children and sacrificed to make sure that we had opportunities that were not afforded to them. My mom was the pillar of strength to our family. Her quiet strength could move mountains, and she loved her family unconditionally. My dad, a carpenter by trade, was a provider. Though strict in his approach, he taught my brothers how to build and how to be resourceful men. Together, my parents taught me how to follow my dreams, overcome adversity and to never give up. "There is nothing you can't do if you keep God first," was their motto.

The foundational principle of faith was the first pillar I learned watching my family navigate the ebbs and flows of life. The family motto was put to test when my dad was shot in Chicago during a home invasion attempt. The tragedy stole my dad's ability to continue with his carpentry business, which led us on a road to Arkansas to live near my dad's parents until he could get back on his feet. As a little girl, this was my first introduction to the power of resiliency in my bloodline.

Living on Ferris Mountain Drive in my grandparents' old house in Fordyce, Arkansas, was one of my earliest memories as a child of having to overcome a mountain of instability. We left a beautiful house and neighborhood in Chicago and shopping trips with my mom to a life where I had only two dresses to wear to school and Christmas gifts were rare. I vividly recall strategically placing buckets around my grandparent's house to catch the rainwater leaking through the roof. There were periods of insecurity, but never did that overshadow the love that was present. My dad made sure we always had food on the table and my mom kept the family unified and made sure our basic needs were met. Looking back, we never lacked for anything of substance. This early experience in life taught me that anything that can be bought with money is not expensive. The things that really mattered were things that money could not buy — love, faith and family.

Living in a house with a shaky foundation, peeling paint, and holes in the roof was my first opportunity to look at a situation in its present condition and dream of what it could be. To the naked eye, what may have appeared to be a shack was much more to me and my family—it was a home. I quickly learned that as a visionary, you must be able to look for possibilities and potential in everything. And my mom was a master at that. She made that tiny two room house feel like a mansion. She filled it with love, and we created everlasting memories. My siblings and I still reminisce about how our mom could make a gourmet meal out of a can of spam and how the aroma of her homemade biscuits could fill your belly and your soul!

Winston Churchill said, "comparison is the thief of all joy," and we never compared ourselves to anyone. Instead, our struggles became the foundation for our success. The healthy since of self that our parents instilled in us gave me the strength, courage and fortitude to become the first African- American homecoming queen at the University of Arkansas at Little Rock, pursue my lifelong ambition and dream to become a lawyer, and lean into my faith when life didn't go as planned.

My dad eventually healed and rekindled his passion for carpentry. He and my brothers would allow me to tag along and pass nails and hold the measuring tape. I was always fascinated with watching them transform houses. They leveled foundations, replaced roofs, added rooms, built from the ground up — you name it, they did it! Through this experience, I was able to witness them take boards, nails, concrete, and regular building materials and transform a mess into masterpiece. I was blown away by the reveal of the completed project. "Is this the same house, I would often ask?!! The time spent with them passing nails taught me ingenuity and imagination, which allowed me to look at a distressed house and imagine its beauty.

My parents were strong proponents of education. My mom, who never graduated high school, taught me the foundation of education and gave me the confidence to dream. Homework was often done by the light of a kerosene lamp when my dad couldn't pay the electricity bill. For me, that was more motivation to succeed so that I could help my family. I was the first of my siblings to go to college with a full scholarship, paving the way for my siblings to follow. We struggled together, shared the same Hershey's chocolate bar, and overcame together. I will be forever grateful for my upbringing.

My mom passed away in 2018. Words can't describe the feeling of losing a parent's touch, love and laughter. It leaves an aching hole in your soul that only a mother can fill. I treasure the years spent with her and all the life lessons that she taught me, especially how to be resilient, how to forgive and how to keep pushing forward and overcome. I remember when one of my brothers drowned during my first year of law school and how the tragedy crushed my family. The paralyzing news flooded my heart with questions of whether I could continue with school. My mom, in the midst of coping with her greatest loss, still found strength to encourage me to finish what I started.

Dementia recently caused my dad to retire his tool belt, but the work ethic that he instilled in me has allowed me to provide for my immediate and extended family. He taught his girls to be independent and to stay in a position to take care of ourselves, even if it means working multiple jobs to have multiple streams of income. All the lessons I learned as a child have carried me through the ebbs and flows in my own life, and I have instilled these same traits in my daughters.

My transition into real estate began in early 2000, after sweating it out in a spin class. I was in the locker room and my gym friend mentioned that she was going to Home Depot to price some cabinets and toilets for a house she was flipping. I threw my head back and laughed at my tall, strikingly beautiful friend, and thought to myself, what could she possibly know about toilets and fixing a house." But my curiosity got the best of me, and I inquired further. She told me how she found a vacant house for sale and secured financing to fix it.

I thought to myself, "I grew up around construction, handing nails and tools to my dad and brothers, so I can surely do this!" So, it was a no-brainer for me when she offered to show me the ropes. Securing my first two vacant properties was a breeze, as was getting approved for a hard money loan. I hired my first contractor and he failed to complete the job. I quickly realized that you can't trust everyone who holds themselves out as a contractor. This revelation forced me back to my roots, and I called my dad and brothers to finish the rehab. The satisfaction I received when I was able to hand the keys to a first-time homeowner made all the trials and tribulations worth it.

After successfully completing a few fix and flips, I was excited about the possibility of scaling my investments in real estate. However, the demands of my legal career, along with raising my small daughters put real estate on the back burner. My daughters are now in college and graduate school pursuing careers in the medical field.

In early 2021, an opportunity to learn the nuts and bolts of investing in single family homes presented itself, and I jumped back into real estate investing with both feet. I joined Wealth Through Real Estate, a mentorship program that really taught me the granular aspects of investing. Through this nine-month intensive program, I learned the art of acquisitions, calculating repair costs, hiring reputable contractors, assessing after repair value, evaluating various exit strategies, and the power of tax advantages in real estate.

With confidence and a solid blueprint before me, I've been able to partner and leverage relationships and do multiple deals at once. In September 2022, I attended a three-day intensive multi-family investment workshop, which again sparked curiosity. I remember listening intently while the presenter explained how to 10x your investment through apartment investing. I immediately thought of the conversation I had with my friend in the gym, and thought, once again, "I can do this!" So, when the speaker asked, "Are you ready to scale your investment business?" I immediately said, "yes." Betting on myself, I raised my hand and wrote the check. Since then, I have invested in over 900 units and I'm just getting started.

I'm not sure if my kids will follow in my footsteps as an active investor, but whether they choose to be active or remain passive, it doesn't matter because real estate is a vehicle to generational wealth. I am creating a legacy for them to continue, if they choose. They embody my grit and determination and I have no doubt that they will excel in life whatever path they take.

I want this chapter to inspire others to not allow their circumstances to cripple them. There will always be obstacles that present themselves, but how you show up and navigate around them will determine what path you end up on. It's not how you start, but how you finish. Real estate has given me the opportunity to start again and navigate life on my terms. That's truly the power of real estate.

Dezette Weathers

Dezette Weathers has been a licensed attorney for 27 years. She earned her bachelor's degree in criminal justice and a Juris Doctor from the University of Arkansas at Little Rock. She has litigated in state and federal court, handling both civil and criminal cases. Her real estate investment career has spanned over two decades. In 2022, she added multifamily investing to her resume, and since then, she has acquired over 900 units as a passive and active investor. Dezette is committed to evolving as an investor and is actively involved in growing her knowledge and community. She is involved in several local and national mastermind groups, including the Brad Sumrock Millionaire Multi-Family Mastermind.

She is an active member of One Community Church and is passionate about sharing her experiences to encourage others as they navigate through life.

Dezette's heartbeats are her two beautiful daughters, Alayna and Symone and Simba, her 12-year-old Akita. She enjoys spending time with her dad and siblings reminiscing about life on Ferris Mountain. They still visit the old house, which her brothers have restored.

 linktr.ee/dezette_weathers

Chapter 6

WHERE HAS REAL ESTATE BEEN MY WHOLE LIFE?

Candius Stearns

I'm a fourth-generation farmer. I grew up where the air was clean, and people relied on God for the harvest. I saw my family work hard and wondered what career path to choose because farming is a hard way to make a living. I wasn't afraid of work but wanted to get paid repeatedly, becoming my life journey to build a passive income stream!

This quest took me on a path of many careers; farming, insurance, travel, politics, and multifamily real estate.

Growing Up on the Farm and Looking For Leverage

Farmers have a serious work ethic. In farm life, if you don't work, you don't eat. That work ethic carried over into every area of my life, thinking, and entrepreneurial endeavors. I quickly learned how my strong work ethic could garner me higher wages than my peers. Here's the rub: trading hours for dollars will only go so far. We all have the same 24 hours a day and seven days a week. I searched for a higher wage through education and specialization at each job, but I wanted a **way to earn money by leveraging time.** Working three jobs and sleeping 4 hours a day didn't cut it!

Build a Successful Business Don't Just Work at One

Dropping out of college eight classes from a 4-year degree in Biology doesn't sound like a success story! My street-smart self told me, though, to get out of college now without debt and stop trading dollars and hours for education you will not get an ROI for.

I worked for an insurance company during college and saw my first career with residual income. I worked with health insurance professionals who made 3 - 5 % of the clients' premiums in the form of a commission each month. The customer paid their monthly bill, and the insurance company paid the agent commission. The light bulb came on; I had found a residual income to leverage my time into dollars.

Two years later, I started an insurance agency and entered the world of entrepreneurship. Within a few years, I had a two million dollar agency and created a compliance company to work with the clients. But the client's income wasn't passive; I still worked many hours. My search continued.

Running for Congress and Running for Your Life

I'm very passionate about God, country, and how our founding fathers crafted the Constitution. Our founding documents are more than just a piece of paper. It's our life, liberty, and pursuit of happiness, not a guarantee of income, but the ability to build and own your own business and property. I grew up valuing God, our Constitution, and our freedoms in my small farm town community. While running my two companies, I experienced the bureaucratic political game, which gets increasingly divisive each political cycle. DC continues to collect our tax dollars and then spends it how they feel. All the while, average Americans are crushed by higher taxes, red tape, and business fees. I got politically involved in 2008 when DC decided to upend the healthcare world. Anytime the government says they're going to fix something, you know we are all in deep trouble.

The attack affected all Americans, and we in the healthcare industry knew it. Insurance agents nationwide read the policy and ran the numbers. One hundred percent of employer groups with 50 or fewer employees would have their premium rates changed from an average single, couple, or family rate to an individual age rate for each family member. No more averaging to make it fair for older people or large families. It's called discrimination! We all knew what was happening. The law turned me into the captain of the Titanic. I hit the iceberg but worked like hell throughout 2010-2013 to send my clients off in the life rafts. 2010 was a turning point in my life where I decided I needed to focus on finding real passive income.

The events with healthcare reform led me to my race for the United States 9th District House of Representatives in 2018. I'm writing a book *Jane Doe Runs for Congress*, about it. I took on Washington because I knew how to fix our broken healthcare system that is destroying the family physically and financially. I had spent ten years lobbying nationally on Capitol Hill with my trade association and felt led by the Lord to do something about it. During my 18 months of campaigning, I connected with individuals, families, and business owners. It ignited my passion for empowering hardworking, salt-of-the-earth farmers, factory workers, and small business owners to take ownership of their financial future. To ensure your future is to create generational wealth, the best way I've found is to leverage your money and time with multifamily real estate!

Spoiler Alert! God didn't have DC in my future, and I lost in 2018. When the race ended, I didn't want to return to the insurance business full-time. I was burnt out and wanted to sell products clients were excited to buy. So I opened a Travel Agency. Everyone loves a great vacation.

In July of 2021, God led me into the investment world. What I thought I knew about real estate was WRONG! Real estate investing was REITs and paper, just like stocks and bonds. I didn't know people like me, "the little guy," could own thousands of units and have an opportunity to become a billionaire. I didn't realize individuals could buy apartments, improve the property (CapX,) and sell them like flipping a single-family home. I finally found a way to leverage money and time. *Where has this been all my life?*

Real Estate The Best Kept Secret?

So, it's the summer of 2021. Everyone's on their boats or up North, and I'm immersing myself in multifamily real estate and the syndication space like I'm cramming for the bar exam. I'm overjoyed and keep asking, "Is this too good to be true?" Why has nobody told me about this before now?

That was my hardest realization entering real estate, just initially seeing that this pencils out and is working for others like me. Obviously, there are scams and cons in every industry, but the people who know what they're doing are helping the 99% of us in the world create equity and build our net worth. Do your due diligence, ask the tough questions, then take massive action!

Fourth Generation Farmer to Multifamily Real Estate

In insurance and financial planning, salespeople sell you their products from their companies and get paid a residual cut of your investment in their products. The salesperson receives payment as your net worth increases.

So why did my financial planner never discuss private placement apartments in my portfolio?

Most investment professionals can't offer these private placement vehicles to you and get paid. Or worse, the financial institution (Broker/ Dealer) won't let them.

How do you then learn about the opportunity?

Research and get to know a syndication team. Syndicates are GPs who do the heavy lifting. A syndication team examines each apartment deal, like buying a business. Suppose the company (apartment) is not running well. The syndication team reviews the Profit and Loss statement, rent rolls, and Net Operating Income to see if their team can improve the balance sheet and bring you a good ROI. It's leveraging your money over time without you having to manage the property!

It's one of the best-kept secrets in the investment world, and you should know about this opportunity to decide if the risk-reward is an option you want to participate in.

All investments are risks, But multifamily real estate can generate generational wealth.

Forget Single Family Homes. It's another Job. We're Going to 10X It!

My husband Chris and I considered doing a single-family fix and flip in the Detroit area around 2008. Chris worked 14 years at Chrysler when the company was going through its third ownership transition, and a buyout package offer landed on his desk. He took the buyout package and moved on from Chrysler, but it was a horrible time to buy single-family homes in Michigan to fix and flip. I'm so glad we did not get into a single-family flipping business. I've learned through experience don't take the bus if you can fly first class to arrive at your destination!

Finding Massive Capital the GP Team

When you're investing in multifamily real estate, it's essential to be working with the right team. The right team knows how to find the deals that work, the right asset manager, and the most profitable numbers. As an investor, I research to partner with the best. Massive Capital had a proven track record, so Christopher and I could sleep well at night. We know our money is working harder than a farmer 24/7.

Too Good to Be True?

Sometimes I ask, "Is this real? Are we doing this?" My hardest realization entering real estate was seeing this pencil out and working for others like me. Every industry has scams and cons, but the people who know what they're doing are helping 99% of us create equity and build our net worth. Do your homework, ask tough questions, take massive action!

Building Equity is How You Create Generational Wealth

In 2022 over 1/2 million people invested in apartment deals. You look at the number, grey-collar employees, attorneys, and doctors. Many do real estate part-time; it just makes sense. What are the key takeaways? Of all asset classes you can hold, multifamily properties are among the best to generate somewhat predictable and routine net operating income with other people's money.

Building equity is how you create generational wealth. You can always make more money. I tell this to my husband. I tell this to everybody. You can always figure out something to sell, trade so many hours for dollars doing something. But real estate gives you something tangible that lasts beyond your years. Like when you purchase a piece of a Class A apartment complex, like, I've done. I can die, and it's still there. It's still going to be rented to whoever moves into the building in the future. The general partner and the asset management teams will continue to find renters make capital improvements to the building, and pull out equity to leverage the money from the apartment to buy another property and repay the initial Capital with a profit to the limited partners who invested in the business plan.

So generational wealth creation is obtainable for you just like it is for me. If you've been wondering, is there another way to generate income without trading your 24 hours a day for dollars? I can assure you there is. People build businesses and go to work every day to support themselves and their families, but what if you could take the money you save and earn and double it every five to 7 years? This is the power of leveraging the money in real estate. Real estate is giving me my hours back so I can spend more time building my life with the ones

I've worked so hard to help provide for! In my opinion, Multifamily real estate investing is a way to give your future generation a nest egg without spending 80 hours every week trading hours for dollars.

Changing People's Lives

Yeah, time is why I got into Multifamily, but now it's also the ability to help other people. I mean, that's my goal now. When I tell people my story about investing, I want to be able to help others do what I'm doing. Even people that work for me in my other businesses. I'm like you guys. Instead of putting all your money into a 401K with who knows what's going on, set some aside and invest in 14 doors or team up with somebody who's already successful doing real estate.

Just the ability to **change people's lives**. I mean, free up time. My husband and I, the first five years we were together, had very little time. We both worked 70-plus hours a week for someone else business. Our time together was basically while we slept or Saturday mornings at the Arthur Murray Dance Studio, where we had dance class together because it was our date morning. He worked afternoons, and I worked days, so we basically had our dates at breakfast and met up at the dance studio to learn how to ballroom dance.

So, if we would have had that kind of passive income, then if I would have known real estate then and even invested $25,000 and turned it into 50,000 and then turned 50,000 into 100K. If we would have had that money early in my life, I wouldn't have had to work while I was breastfeeding. You know what I mean? I wouldn't have had to give up a lot of things that we gave up.

We have a 20-year-old, soon-to-be junior at Michigan State in the fall, and then my youngest is going to be a junior in high school at

Parkway Christian in the fall; he's 16.

Real Estate Helped Us Get on the Same Page

Real estate is something me and my husband can both agree on. I've tried different business ventures over the years. Some turned out well, and some fell flat, but multifamily real estate is something we both can agree on consistently for long-term wealth, and at over 100,000,000 in assets under management with our team, everyone is smiling!

My husband Christopher still thinks I'm a workaholic to this day, and I am probably, but I genuinely love entrepreneurship and real estate, and now I'm helping him reduce his work hours through our passive income stream!

Candius M. Stearns

Candius M. Stearns is an accomplished entrepreneur, business-woman, and real estate investment professional. With a remarkable track record of success, she has established herself as a trusted name in the industry.

As the founder and CEO of Stearns HR, formerly DFBenefits Inc, Candius has revolutionized employee benefits and HR compliance for small businesses. Passionate about travel and delivering exceptional experiences, Candius owns Stay Balanced Travel, a unique travel agency specializing in curating luxury destinations and tailor-made itineraries for busy business owners and C-suite managers who want balance in their life and work.

In addition to her involvement in employee benefits and travel, Candius is a partner of Massive Capital, an esteemed investment firm. Massive Capital has gained recognition for its strategic investments and impressive growth. Candius's keen business acumen and leadership contribute to the firm's success, establishing it as a prominent player in the investment landscape. With an impressive portfolio valued at $110 million, she possesses extensive knowledge and expertise in identifying lucrative investment opportunities, developing strategic partnerships, and managing assets effectively. Her dedication to excellence, meticulous attention to detail, and commitment to building long-term relationships with investors make her an invaluable asset in the real estate investment industry.

Candius M. Stearns continues to significantly contribute to the business world through her innovative ventures, entrepreneurial spirit, and dedication to excellence. With her diverse skill set and unwavering determination, she is a true inspiration for aspiring entrepreneurs and investors alike.

We simplify real estate investing for busy professionals to create wealth by acquiring ownership of income-producing properties.

Contact me here at my linktr.ee/candius

Chapter 7

GOD'S GRACE FOR ANOTHER PLACE

Cecilia Cossio

It wasn't easy being 17 and pregnant in the '80s. I knew life would be tough but I would figure it out. I would not give in or give up and I made the decision that I was going to do greater things.

Teen Mom to Real Estate Operator & Investor

I found myself thrust into the daunting role of a mother while still grappling with the challenges of my own teenage years. It was an overwhelming struggle, but I was determined to stay focused on my future.

There were countless nights when I burned the midnight oil, juggling textbooks and bottles, determined to carve out a path for us. Early mornings were met with tired eyes, but my love for my family fueled a deep sense of purpose. Hard work became my constant companion as I toiled tirelessly to provide for my growing family and create a stable foundation. My dream of financial freedom and a better life would not be realized for years to come, I was determined and believed that one day **faith, family, hard work, and desire would help me create a legacy.**

Leaving the country to live in Europe due to my ex's military obligations was not easy at 18, but my grandfather reminded me in order to grow, you must experience what others have not. Grandpa told me to keep learning and pushing myself to get my college degree and, above else, when scared, pray. I learned to overcome challenges without excuses and believed that I could accomplish anything if I wanted it bad enough.

With two marriages ending in divorce, you wonder how to make it through the pain and uncertainty without hurting your children any more than you already have. There were things that were not supposed to happen, but I always turned to my faith, and God's provision never failed me. I could go back and write a book on these last-minute miracles that were stacking up. In fact, that would be a cool book title: "Last Minute Miracles." I was always grateful for the people God put in our life, especially those that left us too soon. Even though I didn't know it at the time, they were an answer to our prayers. Now that the tables have turned, we get the chance to be the Good Samaritans and pay it forward for someone else and that is part of the legacy I am supposed to leave behind.

As the years passed, I transformed from a young girl burdened with responsibility into an empowered single mother. My journey was not without self-inflicted hiccups, but it is a testament to the power of faith, family and hard work. Today, I stand tall, grateful for the lessons learned and the resilience forged in the fire of adversity. My story is one of triumph over struggle, and I am determined to pass down this legacy of strength and perseverance to my children, inspiring them to reach for their own dreams, no matter the obstacles they may face.

My Kids are My Motivation

My kids, Bianca (34), EJ (28), and Joseph (15), are the driving force behind every step I take in life. I believe, as mothers, we are all hard-wired with a unique instinct to care for and nurture our children. From the moment they entered my life, they became my reason, my drive, and my motivation. Their smiles, their laughter, and their unwavering love for family fuel my determination to create a better future for them. They have witnessed my struggles and triumphs, and their unwavering support has been my guiding light. The joy I feel in watching them grow and thrive motivates me to work harder, dream bigger, and never give up. My kids are not only the recipients of my love but also the source of my strength and inspiration. They remind me every day of the legacy I am building, and I am grateful for the blessing of being their mother. Bianca, EJ, and Joseph remind me daily of how far we have come, and my grandkids -- Michaela, Maddie, Isaac, Eric, Mason, Evalyn, Tre, and Eli (ages 9-19) – give me hope for the future.

My greatest victory is the love my children have for each other. Yeah, that's been my greatest victory. The real estate, the deals, all of that is great, but that's just my day job. My kids are my greatest blessings. I see how they've turned out, and that gives me the most joy.

With every grandbaby I've held in my arms, I've cried and thanked the Lord. I've thought about them, looked them in the eyes, and said, "I had a tough start in life, but I'm going to give you something that nobody gave me, and that is a financial education, love, and an opportunity to be and do anything you want." Thanks to my grandparents, I decided not to become a statistic. I chose life, and that has helped me make so many of the other right choices. I never gave up, and I'm just getting started!

Raised by the Most Amazing Grandparents

I was blessed to be raised by the most amazing grandparents, who stepped in and became my parents. They selflessly took on the responsibility of guiding me through life, providing the love and support I needed. Even though I come from a very humble background, thanks to my grandparents and uncles, I never went without. To me, they are not just grandparents; they are my pillars of strength and unwavering role models. Their nurturing presence instilled in me a deep sense of faith, both through their words and their actions. Their belief in me has shaped the person I am today, and I am eternally grateful for the values and principles they imparted. I know in my heart that they are proud of the person I have become, and I strive every day to make them proud. Their unconditional love, guidance, and example have been the cornerstone of my life, and I am forever grateful for the gift of being raised by the most amazing grandparents.

Hard Work, Faith, and Family

My grandparents always modeled hard work for me. They were always supportive but did not give me a free pass. I was also always determined to improve my family's situation. I chose to drop out of high school twice to provide income and keep working but was able to finally finish, get my diploma and focus on full-time work. I studied for my college courses through VHS tapes that were mailed to us.

I started out as a part-time property leasing agent and worked my way up to become the president of the company. But I always had in my mind that I was going to quit working for everyone else one day and start working for myself.

Property Management to Multifamily Real Estate

I've been in the property management space for 30 years. I'm the president of a property management company, so through my growth, I've just seen the money I make everybody else. I eventually resolved that it was time to start making my own. Fifteen years ago, I was able to participate in the profit-sharing equity of the real estate deals through my company, but it wasn't until three years ago that I began investing a portion of my monthly income into multifamily real estate. I think it was Jim Rohn who said, "Equity is better than wages," and I agree! Knowing that I'm leveraging a growing portion of my monthly income into a solid, appreciating asset like multifamily real estate makes me feel good.

Create Lasting Legacy – Investing in Myself

Time freedom, security, and creating lasting wealth for myself and my heirs are the things I wrote down on my dream board in my 20s. It's taken me a moment to get here, but I can say we are doing it, and we are getting closer to the realization of that goal every day. Most people never start because they can't start big, so they don't start at all. I say start where you are, be consistent, and let God help you with the rest. A little bit over time makes a big difference with diligence.

Most people work for a company; few people work for themselves. In multifamily real estate, your investment is working for you, but you don't have to micromanage it every day. Today, I'm a limited partner, and I look at those units as residual income streams that pay me month in and month out while also appreciating. These assets give me the best tax deductions and long-term wealth. As I grow my wealth through real estate, I feel confident knowing my investments are recession-proof, always appreciating, and giving me incredible tax advantages!

Giving Women Hope and an Opportunity

In the world of multifamily real estate, I have found my calling - not only as a single mom but also as a passionate advocate for giving women hope and opportunities. Through my journey, I have witnessed firsthand the challenges and barriers women face in this industry. It has fueled my determination to create a pathway for them to succeed. I firmly believe that every woman deserves a chance to thrive, regardless of their background or circumstances. By providing mentorship, resources, and a supportive network, I aim to empower women and equip them with the tools they need to excel in multifamily real estate.

In my endeavors, I am driven by the belief that women bring unique perspectives, skills, and talents to this field. I am dedicated to fostering an environment where they can thrive, break through glass ceilings, and create a legacy. By offering educational opportunities, networking events, and access to resources, I strive to level the playing field and empower women to take charge of their financial futures.

I have seen firsthand the transformative power of giving women hope and an opportunity in multifamily real estate. It not only changes their lives but also ripples out to impact their families, communities, and generations to come. I am committed to championing women, uplifting their spirits, and showing them that with determination, hard work, and the right support system, they can achieve greatness. Together, we can shatter barriers, defy expectations, and create a more inclusive and prosperous future in the multifamily real estate industry.

"My greatest reward in this business is when an employee, customer, or investor thanks me for how I've changed their life!"
– Cecilia Cossio

Cecilia Cossio

Cecilia is a dynamic and accomplished professional, excelling in the realm of real estate. With an extensive 30-year tenure in property management, she has garnered invaluable expertise across diverse asset classes, effectively overseeing the management of 5,000+ units. As a testament to her unwavering belief in real estate investments, Cecilia not only operates as a full-time real estate operator and investor but also invests her own capital and dedicates her personal time to lucrative deals. Her exceptional journey to success is marked by resilience and determination in the face of adversity. From overcoming the challenges of being a teenage mother, Cecilia has proven her ability to conquer obstacles that may have deterred others. Her unwavering spirit and faith have been guiding forces during difficult times, consistently fueling her drive to succeed. Cecilia firmly believes in the transformative power within every individual, regardless of their background or the obstacles they encounter. Her personal growth and wealth of experience have fueled her aspiration to share her knowledge with others, specifically in the realm of multifamily investments and the pursuit of financial freedom. A captivating and influential professional, Cecilia seeks to empower individuals, imparting valuable insights and guiding them toward a prosperous future. With a stellar track record, unyielding determination, and a deep commitment to personal growth, Cecilia is an invaluable asset for anyone seeking expert guidance in the realm of real estate and financial success.

Chapter 8

FINANCING YOUR DREAMS TO FINANCIAL FREEDOM

Kim Pokuta-Ramirez

Speaking on Grant Cardone's 10X Real Estate Summit Stage

Coming off the stage at Grant's premier real estate event in 2021, I found myself getting mobbed by dozens of real estate investors armed with business cards, questions, and smartphones poised to record. Not only was I surrounded by what seemed like hundreds of new investors asking questions about real estate financing, but they all wanted my card. I said, "Well, my bank doesn't know I'm here right now, so I'll give you my cell." That night, I was followed for hours like a celebrity with paparazzi in tow, fielding inquiries, accepting business cards, and posing for selfies.

I began to realize after the last after-after party that my short-lived fame would not be dying down anytime soon. I went home not only with 100+ new close friends and joint venture partners, but I also met an investor in Southern California who brought me $11 million in business over the next 12 months. My VIP ticket upgrade had been covered and then some!

On the second day of the summit, I was sitting up front in the VIP section, and Grant asked, "Questions, who has a question?" I raised my hand, and Grant called on me. "Hi, what's your name, and where are you from?

"My name is Kim Pakula Ramirez; I'm from Southern California. I'm a commercial lender."

"You're a commercial lender? Oh my God, get up on stage!"

Grant immediately brought me on stage to ask me questions in real time about lending with an audience of 3,000+ people at the Turnberry Marriott in Aventura, Florida – in addition to over 10,000+ people watching the summit virtually as it was live streaming.

My mind flashed back to the first day when I considered for two seconds, "Should I upgrade to VIP for five figures?" I figured, "I'm here, so I might as well get the best seat in the house." They said he called on VIPs during the Q&A time, and I had my questions ready. As I drifted off to sleep at 2:23 am that night, a smile crossed my face as I rehearsed it in my thoughts.

From a Knack for Numbers to $288 Million in Real Estate Funded

You learn some amazing things about yourself growing up in a home with two alcoholic parents. I quickly learned my strengths and weaknesses. I loved math, and I was great at calculus, so I went into finance in college and got hired at Wells Fargo, and the rest, as they say, is history. Even then, I always seemed to have a gift for making money multiply.

Wells Fargo chose me as one of the 50 new employees from a pool of 1,000 applicants. That was a happy day for me. I started out as a small business banker, then quickly moved up to be an underwriting manager and grew my department from three to 17 employees.

After five years, I got a little burned out with it. I thought, "You know what? I know how to build relationships. I have the underwriting background, and I know the ins and outs. I need to be a wholesale account executive and go meet with the brokers and show them how to structure their deals." So, I took over this account that was giving the bank $400,000, and I turned it into a 4 million client. From my second year, I was number four out of 320 reps nationwide. The top three were men; I was the top female out of 320. I doubled, then tripled my income, making crazy amounts of money, and bought my million-dollar-plus home – before the meltdown of 2008 happened.

Dreams of Financial Freedom

I bought my first house when I was 27. I wanted financial freedom for myself. I wanted to control my own future. I've always been goal-oriented, and over the last few years, I've done personal development, mentoring, and coaching. I believe in manifestation. I've been a student of *Think and Grow Rich* since I was in my twenties.

I had done transformational courses, and then I got Jim Fortin's *Transform Your Life* in 2019. I did his program, and it lived up to its promise: I began to transform! Vision boards are something I've always had up on my wall and my mirrors. I wrote down my dreams and goals and manifested them. I've always kept my dreams and goals in front of me, checking myself periodically against my progress and removing what was holding me back.

Corporate Success to Personal Freedom

It occurred to me early on that if I was working for corporate, I was making someone else's company rich. To truly have personal freedom, I needed to build my own real estate portfolio.

I'm a passive investor now with Grant Cardone. I have 686 units that I'm an investor in. I'm getting monthly residual income off that, and that's cool. The thing that excites me the most about being a passive investor with him is that as I continue to build my portfolio, eventually, I'll be able to replace my income, and then I'll be completely financially free. I've taken steps, and I'm on my way. Now I'm living my dream and just a 15-minute walk from the Pacific Ocean.

Network Your Way to Success

I've always been a natural networker. I've had a knack since I was a teenager for walking into a room and starting to matchmake, putting people together to solve each other's problems. I think it's something I was born with, and I'm grateful for it. It's really helped me in business and in life. Being a go-giver is just second nature to me. I've always found that when I pay it forward, it always comes back to me in positive ways. I won a 45-minute ride on Grant's luxury helicopter (Bird) over the coast of Miami not long after I met him and shared the stage with him. I was the only female and felt like I was living the life of the rich and famous - truly an incredible experience. That event continues to open doors for me on a weekly basis.

Speaking From Stage Helps You Connect Quickly

I've heard that people do business with people they know, like, and trust, and for me, the fastest way to collapse the trust curve is to get on stage and be seen as the expert. I have given hundreds of talks and presentations to small groups over the course of my career, but what I learned coming off Grant Cardone's stage was the exponential power of being a speaker and gaining trust quickly with your target audience in the room. That is networking on steroids, and I plan to do a lot more of it, not only speaking on physical stages at events but also on podcasts, webinars, and virtual events.

Not only did I find the $11 million from that stage, but I now have a Rolodex of new friends who are as eager to help as I am. We've created many mini communities that serve one another as we grow in our multifamily journey together. I get calls weekly from the people at met at this event or the people I was introduced to because of being on stage and speaking at this event. In fact, that's why I'm in this book – thanks, Brooke Ceballos-Pinero!

My Soulmate Journey

This past year, I set my intention to find my soulmate. It's been a great learning experience as I've grown deeper as a person and really gotten to know myself. I've been able to come to terms with who I am and what I'm looking for at this stage in my life. I have a feeling it won't be long before I manifest my soulmate. Who knows, he might be reading this chapter right now!

Funding Your Dreams in Multifamily

Real estate deals are as diverse as your thumbprint. Every deal is different; every state is different; every investor is different. You must know what transactions, loans, and team is right for you.

I've been in banking my whole life. I've been a lender, a residential mortgage lender, and a commercial lender. For my entire working career, I've been on this quest to finance dreams of financial freedom. With all the relationships and resources I have at my disposal, it's been so rewarding helping these amazing women I've recently met get funded with the right solution for them and their deal. With my diverse lending background, we can get most people funded with some creative financing and proper structuring. I've funded over $288 million in loans in my career.

Women who are reading the book right now may have found a deal and now are asking, "Who will be the lender? Which bank is going to finance this loan?" I feel like that's where I come into play. I'll be able to help them because I have contacts nationwide. If you are doing fix-and-flips or wholesale or residential or multifamily, I can help you. I've got broker friends that lend within all 50 states, so I can evaluate the type of deal and matchmake based on its criteria. Jump on my calendar, and let's talk.

My Book Coming Out in 2024

I have two amazing kids. I have a 24-year-old daughter, Taylor, and a 20-year-old son Anthony. Anthony will be 21 in August. Taylor graduated from Pepperdine. She has her dream career in the music industry and lives in West Hollywood on her own. My son's transferring to a university and plans to go into film. Both of my kids are great. I am so proud of them, and I know they are very proud of me too!

I just know that I have this bigger purpose, and I'm going to touch more lives. I feel this book is going to open the door to additional opportunities, and maybe this is how I leave corporate America. I'm going on a trip to Italy in September to finish my book. I can't wait to bring more of my story to the world in 2024!

What Do You Say to Yourself at 65?

So, here you are. You're on the back porch. You're 65, and you're with your soulmate. You're having a glass of wine and reflecting on your life. What is the message you share with yourself? How do you feel about what you've accomplished?

I'm complimenting myself for pursuing my passion for financial freedom and achieving my dreams. My advice to the younger version of myself would be to invest more in multifamily real estate early and take half of what I was putting into my 401K and diversify that into real estate. But overall, I'm very proud of what I've been able to accomplish. I look at my soulmate and tell him how grateful I am that God brought him into my life, and we start planning our next vacation in Europe and my speaking tour in the USA.

I feel like my purpose in life is to help people and make a positive difference in their lives.

Jump on my calendar now, and let's collaborate. I can't wait to meet you! Email me at KPREInvestLLC@gmail.com

---

Kim Pokuta-Ramirez

Kim Pokuta-Ramirez is a Vice President-Relationship Manager with a regional bank in California and is responsible for managing over 50 clients. Drawing on more than 30 years of commercial/mortgage banking experience in management, underwriting, and business development, Kim and her team of financial specialists work to deliver strategic financial solutions and guidance to their clients. Clients are businesses throughout Orange County and Los Angeles with annual sales revenue of $10 - $200 million. Representative clients include manufacturers, wholesalers, distributors, health care, contractors, and privately held businesses. The banking needs of these businesses and organizations can range from basic to highly complex.

Core capabilities include long-term fixed-rate commercial financing (conventional and SBA 504), working capital lines of credit, equipment financing, treasury management, and merchant processing. The team excels at combining leading-edge technology with a high level of personalized service and business acumen. Kim and her team are also equipped to assist with customized corporate card programs, foreign exchange, letters of credit, and interest rate hedges.

Kim is a graduate of California State University Fullerton, where she earned her B.A. in Finance. Kim sits on the Board of Directors for Second Chance Orange County (SCOC) and is also involved with the Association for Corporate Growth (ACG) and Risk Management Association (RMA). In addition, Kim also volunteers at Promise Scholars, Feeding America, and Habitat for Humanity. Kim enjoys art museums, theater, jazz, dining, and traveling, along with spending quality time with her two adult children and close friends. Email me at KPREInvestLLC@gmail.com

SCAN ME

Chapter 9

HIGHLY PAID DOCTOR LIVING FROM PAYCHECK TO PAYCHECK CASHES IN ON MULTIFAMILY REAL ESTATE

Dr. Olayinka Holt

I grew up in Nigeria. We were poor but I didn't know we were poor. We were loved and that's what mattered. Life was hard but for a young child that had a dream - nothing was going to stop me. I had a dream.

I had a dream to be a doctor and help people. Rising through the obstacles of a male-dominated world first in Nigeria and then in the USA to become who I am today as an independent successful physician, single mother, real estate investor, and entrepreneur has been my unique journey.

My earliest dream was to be a doctor and help people. I made the decision to come to the USA when my babies were young because the medical education system in Nigeria is not fair. As a medical student applicant, even with high grades it's easy to get passed over because the other student waiting to take your spot comes from a family with money and your spot is gone, regardless of your grades.

Additionally, even though my babies were little and I didn't have any support I had to leave my husband. He had started another family and told me he would never give up his "new wife" for us. I would have to play second place as my kids grew and that would just rip our hearts out daily. It was one of the toughest decisions I'd have to make, but I never regretted it. God has more than provided for us and we are now, and always have been a strong family that loves and supports one another.

My Faith Would See Me Through

Some people become victims of their environment. But I learned to maintain a vision for my life. My vision came from my faith and from my parent's love. Ever since I was a young child I knew I was born to do something great.

"Where there is no vision the people perish." Proverbs 29:18

My faith is very real and personal to me and it has sustained me throughout my life. When my environment did not line up with the vision in my heart I continued to believe in my vision and press on knowing, eventually, with God's help I was going to make it happen. It wasn't easy and things did not change overnight, it took time. It took years and I'm still climbing the ladder and I will never quit!

Real Estate in Nigeria

I started in 2016 back home in Nigeria, and I built a 16-unit apartment from scratch. Things worked well for awhile. But after coming to the US I'd soon realize there wasn't much profit by the time I paid for a property manager and did the currency conversion so I began to focus on investing in the real estate market in the US. I would, shortly, get to try my hand at investing in the USA without having to worry about property managers, currency conversions, contractors and the like. Sure I feel good that I'm providing quality and affordable housing to families who benefit but it's difficult to manage multifamily to scale in a country you're not living in.

Managing a Mountain of Debt

It can be discouraging when you start your real estate investment journey with a mountain of debt, but I was determined. When I graduated, from my fellowship, I was employed. And at that time, I started with a $450,000 medical school loan. And on top of that, I didn't know any better, I added another loan, I bought a house for $325,000. And my salary at the time was only $270,000. So I'm looking at the whole thing, and I'm saying how on earth, will I ever be done with all these loans?

I clearly needed something else to supplement my income especially since I'm getting taxed about 35 to 40% on my income, so by the time I add the taxes to my income, and then I pay my school loan, I pay my mortgage, I pay medical insurance. And my two kids were in college at the time, even though they were getting financial aid, there wasn't enough, I found myself living from paycheck to paycheck. Most doctors I graduated with were in this same boat and many of my doctor friends began living on lines of credit just to make ends meet. I was NOT going to do that. if you feel like you can't afford to do anything now, you can start with something.

Real Estate as a Tax Strategy

That's when I went to my first real estate seminar to learn how to leverage real estate as a tax strategy. But it's not just doctors and those in the medical profession. If you don't have a tax strategy, you're losing

35-45% to taxes every year, year over year to taxes. As I researched real estate like you'd research a virus in the lab, my hypothesis began to prove out; the fastest way to true wealth is multifamily real estate. The more I researched and did my due diligence the more clear it was to me that multifamily real estate would be my vehicle of choice to build long term wealth for me and my kids but that it should also be a part the portfolio of every family in the USA that want true financial freedom.

Single Family to Multi Family

Sizing up my debt and my tax situation I realized something, I need to get rich fast because when you're not investing in multifamily you get crushed with taxes. The tax incentives alone for investing in Class A multifamily real estate make it worth it to me. Not to mention appreciation, leveraging debt, cash flowing properties and so many other benefits. The tax incentive is a little-known secret and any smart professional should not only have money in the stock market and precious metals but should be invested in multifamily real estate. Getting rich slow just did not make sense for me.

Speaking to Women Speaking to Doctors

So as a limited partner, with 2,085 doors right now. I am now an operator. My first General Partner project was 63 units that we're closing on very soon in Dallas.

When I when I get on stage, I promote women and freedom. I want women to be strong. To make their voice known to make their impact known. Ladies, you can do anything. Whatever you set your mind to do you can achieve, don't ever give up, do not quit!

When I speak to medical students or doctors I talk to them about using real estate as a tax strategy like I did then I give them an opportunity to invest in my multifamily deals.

In medical school nobody teaches us the business aspect of medicine – they didn't teach us investing. When I get on stage the first thing I teach them is how to invest and how to make their money work for them.

But I wasn't alone. Most of the doctors I knew were in the same boat with debt, student loans, interest, living on lines of credit, working until they die and never enjoying their retirement.

I began to realize as I talked to the other Doctors I graduated with and those that graduated in the last five years, I was shocked to learn they were ALL living on lines of credit. Let that sink in! That is unsustainable! Not only are you upside down, your boat is capsizing.

Why I Got Into Medicine

Becoming a doctor and helping people was my lifelong dream but when I lost my sister because there was no electricity in my home country to power her dialysis machine that angered me further to the point of taking action. In Nigeria we lack electricity, we lack good water, we lack good air, all our air is polluted. The political system is unstable. And if you don't have money, you don't have good medical treatment. She had a master uterine hemorrhage, went into shock, coma, kidney failure, was started on dialysis. And because there was no electricity to power the dialysis machine, she died. So now that only made my WHY stronger. Because I've always wanted to serve people, I've always wanted to be a physician, and help people feel better. That has always been from way back when I was little. But unfortunately, when I was in Nigeria, at that time, when you graduate from high school, there's a national exam that you take. And if you don't match into your first choice for the career that you wanted, you wait for the second choice. Unfortunately, by the time where I came from, for the second choice, the collection in Nigeria, you already put some rich kid from a rich family, in my spot and I miss out. And that's why I couldn't go to medical school in Nigeria.

But imagine, I came to United States, and I'm a single parent. And I'm thinking of going to medical school. How do I go to medical school as a single parent with two little kids? I kept on applying. And when I found out that I can go to medical school, when I get accepted. But I can't go now because my kids are little. I kept on doing any and every kind of job that I could find, while simultaneously started my pre-med. I decided that when my kids were old enough to take care of their activities of daily living, that's when I'm going to go to medical school. My goal was when my son becomes six, and my daughter is eight, and they can take a shower by themselves, they can clothe themselves, they can make breakfast, or maybe even lunch by themselves, then that's the time I'm going to go to medical school.

Single Mom Raising Wise and Industrious Children

When they were six and eight years old, they can do all of that. My daughter will go to the grocery store and pick up the groceries. They can make breakfast, they can fry eggs for themselves, they can do everything. I taught them hard work and responsibility from an early age, just like I had learned at home.

My dad was a very hard-working man. He started his own business. When I was about eight years old, my dad would ask me to balance his books. I did very well with book-keeping and balancing his books. He made me a signatory to his business accounts. My dad would always tell us that hard work is the foundation of success.

I was fortunate to be smart, and I went through elementary school and high school was a breeze. I was also able to get into college at a very young age and graduated before I was 19 years old. I lived in extreme poverty most of these years. I wore old dresses in college, I had few toiletries, and little to no cash. But that didn't stop my strong belief to become someone in life. I was able to obtain a master's degree in organic chemistry and pursued a PhD in organic chemistry.

Later in the USA my extreme dedication to my calling could be observed by my intense daily schedule; earning 28 credits in just nine months while I was working full-time and raising my two children.

I would work all night from midnight to 8:30am, drive 30 minutes to my school, I start class at nine o'clock in the morning, I finish at one o'clock in the afternoon, I drive two hours to go back home, pick up my children from school, go home, do homework with them and everything, dropped them at the babysitter's house to sleep then I go back to sleep two to three hours max. And I did that for three years, until I got everything taken care of.

So, I'm grateful to God, for everything that I've done especially being a single parent, and my children, seeing how we grew from nothing to something that helped to shape their life also, and they've already adopted my work ethic that I wanted them to know that they must work hard, but they also must work smart. And if they want things, they need to earn their money for those things. I taught them that nothing is going to be handed to them on a platter - You must go get it! My Oldest daughter will be 30 this year Yinka Sarayi, Jide Sarayi is 28 and Ojeifo Okhiria is 14.

Medical School in Belize

I was on the list and waiting to get into medical school in New York and I had a professor give me some of her wisdom, "*Yinka, when you are on the list, anybody that scores higher than you on the MCAT, will drop you down on that list. So even though they're telling you they only accept 70 in a year. You have about four years to wait, if somebody keeps dropping you every time that four years is not realistic. So, if you add four years to your age, now you're going to be more than 40 years old, the average age of retiring in America is 65. How many years are you going to be able to work as a doctor before you retire? If I were you, I know you're very smart woman I know you can live and you can function anywhere, I will encourage you to investigate these offshore schools, like the Caribbean medical schools, get accepted, finish your medicine, come back to United States do the USMLE Examination which is the main exam that every foreign grad does. And once you do that exam, you have the equivalent of an American medical graduate. And that's the end of it.*" Once I verified what she was telling me was correct, that's exactly what I did. So, by that summer, I was finishing my physics. And I started applying to all these offshore schools. And I was lucky - I got accepted in Belize.

I went to school in Belize and sent my children to Nigeria to go stay with my mom, at least for the first four years of medicine. My kids were here up until I did my pre-med. And then when I came back, I passed my exams, and I started residency. That's when I brought them back to come stay with me.

My Promise to God

When I was going to medical school, I started at age 36. I was the oldest in my class. And by that time, I was already more than 10 years out of school, which was not going to be easy to go back and study medicine the way it's supposed to be studied. As a Christian I fasted and prayed. And I made a covenant with God that if you see me through medical school, and I graduate and I pass and I start practicing, I'm going to dedicate some days out of the week, or some months out of the year and go with a mobile clinic with my medical crew and go to the less privileged cities where they don't have health care and provide free health care to everybody. I'm finally able to do this and have some outreaches planned soon.

My Advice To The Younger Version of Myself

My advice to me or any reader is to start with multifamily investing earlier. Even if I only a little bit at first. At Promeritinvestments.com we allow investors to get started with $50,000. Fifty thousand in real estate is much safer and smarter than $50,000 in the stock market. I want you to be able to go on vacation, I want you to be able to live a good life and want you to be healthy. The peace of mind a multifamily investment can give you like ours is worth its weight in gold!

I want to meet you and see if we can work together to build your dreams. Jump on my calendar at: **https://connect.promeritcapital.com/**

Dr. Olayinka Holt

Dr. Olayinka Holt is an accredited investor and the Principal of ProMerit Investments LLC, a private equity firm. She is a single mother of three children; number 9 of 13 children from her father. She relocated to the U.S.A. in 1992 after completing her elementary school through university education in Ibadan, Oyo State Nigeria. At age 16, she got admission to the University of Ibadan where she majored in chemistry and minored in zoology; graduating with her bachelor's degree at the young age of 19. She is a board-certified physician and sole proprietor of a successful medical clinic. Since 2012 she has been serving the South Texas community, which she is very passionate about. Her mission is to inspire and empower migrant women across the US to courageously follow their dreams. In her spare time, she enjoys watching movies, cooking, and taking scenic drives with her children. Dr. Holt's book *THE WALK - Though She Be But Little, She Is Fierce* coming out this fall published by Beyond Publishing Frisco, TX. Dr. Holt is available for speaking and media interviews.

Dr. Olayinka can be reach at: *promeritinvestments.com*

Chapter 10

POVERTY TO PEACE WITH COMMERCIAL REAL ESTATE IMPACT INVESTING

Steph Doblosky

My Story

I didn't come from wealth. I was born to two teenage parents in New Jersey before the internet. Our first family home was a room over a garage and was provided as a favor from a family friend, who also bought us groceries. My Polish American father, in charge of income, barely slept from working three different jobs around the clock to support us. Yet, we still qualified for government assistance. To this day, he has a divot in his left arm from donating blood weekly for extra money to buy groceries. Whenever he extends his arm, I physically see the love he has for me.

My Italian American mother, in charge of cutting expenses, raised me and my little brother. Our daily lives included coupon clipping, taking one-minute lukewarm showers, and wearing nothing but thrift clothing. We tasted grapes in the grocery store before checking out, waited for old bread from the back of the bakery, and ate lots of pasta and peanut butter and jelly. As a family, we were constantly pushing our car to the gas station after it ran out of gas. At home, we snuggled together under blankets during chilly winters and took turns fanning each other with homemade paper fans in hot summers. If I wanted something, I knew not to ask because the answer would be no. I didn't know we were in poverty. I just knew that I was different, and I got free lunch at school.

I vividly remember the moment when I learned the extent of poverty. I was sitting on the floor flipping through a library copy of National Geographic Magazine and stumbled on a picture of a Namibian mother holding her malnourished and dying four-year-old daughter. The magazine pages slowly became stained with my newly seven-year-old teardrops. As I wept, the pages slowly stuck together from my grief and righteous anger. I knew that if I were simply born in a different place, I could be this starving girl. I was in awe of how blessed I was to still be alive at that moment, yet how robbed I would feel if I weren't. I could not comprehend why anyone was starving in such an abundant world.

That was the moment that I knew what poverty was. Right then, I swore two things to myself. One, I would learn everything about what caused this little girl's suffering. Two, I would create incredible wealth to help eliminate this injustice from our world. Thus, my "why" was born. The problem was, I didn't know much about either topic, and I was a poor child myself.

Eventually, since we were a military family, my parents were able to purchase a fixer-upper house with no money down using a VA loan. Whenever we moved, my parents would rent out the house we once lived in and purchase another home. We moved often, repeating the process. Over time, I saw how our lifestyle went from worry to peace, and no turned into yes. I went from the free lunch program to the reduced lunch program. Eventually, I had to pay for lunch. The awkward moments of asking my friends' moms to sponsor me for school field trips slowly went away. I saw the power of passive income with my own eyes. I knew that there was something about real estate that grew wealth. By the time I was ready for college, we were living in a suburban home much like what we had called "rich people's houses" nearly 15 years earlier. Real estate and discipline elevated our family to the upper middle class.

The profit from my parent's first rental property, which was a fixer-upper and the one we could never get all the glitter off the ceilings, sent me to George Mason University. There, I earned my Bachelor of Science in Civil, Environmental, and Infrastructure Engineering. I was the first of our family to graduate from higher education. As an engineer, I learned how vital water, environment, and infrastructure help people gain health and wealth on an individual micro and macro scale. As I donated my engineering skills to developing countries, I understood that I would need to stop trading time for money if I were to leap into abundant wealth and have the greatest impact.

As an engineer, I saw my mentors, very smart and respected individuals, live for their weekends and lose their retirement savings in the Great Recession. They needed to work another ten years, at least, to repair the damage that the recession did to their life savings. I knew that there had to be another way. As a civil engineer in real estate development, I saw real estate developers consistently cutting checks well over $1,000,000. I knew they were on to something based on what my parents taught me about real estate. I later mirrored their single-family rental success with Section 8 tenants but knew there had to be a more scalable solution to grow wealth faster.

It spurred me to earn a Master of Real Estate Development from the University of Maryland, which is essentially the business of commercial real estate. Here, I learned that developers do not start off with $1,000,000 in their pocket. Instead, they use other people's money to invest in development. I also learned that nearly 97% of the wealthiest people on earth invest in real estate in some fashion to preserve their wealth due to the unrivaled tax advantages.

The best tax advantages come from commercial real estate investing, where it is possible to invest in offices, apartment buildings (multifamily), hotels, retail buildings, mobile home parks, industrial buildings, and self-storage units. They are all very different markets and have different demands. One of my favorite investments is multifamily because, like water, it involves investing in a physiological need: shelter. Multifamily has strong market demand for at least another 50 years, as younger generations are priced out of home ownership and boomers downsize. Only behind food, shelter is usually ones of the highest priorities for payment.

Multifamily real estate not only has strong demand, but it has the best bang for its buck when it comes to tax advantages. There are many tax tools in multifamily and commercial real estate, like depreciation, cost segregation, bonus depreciation, tax credits, mortgage insurance deduction, and capital gains tax avoidance, to name a few. Essentially, all these accounting tools, which can be mixed and matched together like nearly no other investment, create a legal tax shelter. That means that you can get all the returns on your investment without legally having to owe taxes on it. You see, the wealthiest know how to keep their money. They do pay some taxes, but they know the rules of the game to avoid their tax burden. Commercial real estate investing is one of the rules. By generating substantial cash flow from passive commercial real estate investing sources and using passive multifamily investing as a tax shelter, generational wealth becomes a real possibility.

I found my path to connecting investors to commercial real estate investments, which are diversified, asset-based, and can create scalable environmental and social change. All my education and my dedication to ending poverty set me apart in this real estate investing space. I have a unique perspective as a civil engineer and a real estate professional. To me, investing is not simply a method of growing financial wealth. Sure, that is important. However, what does that investment do to our world? What impact does it have on poverty? On climate? On social structure? On health? There must be a way that we can have it all.

I look at my investments from three different perspectives. One, who is the team? Two, what are the financial returns? Three, what is the social impact? If the investment meets my criteria, I alert my investors. Then, as investor relations lead, I help my investors get onboarded into the investment and provide timely asset updates throughout the investment holding period.

Team

In any investing process, the team you invest with can be your biggest asset or your biggest risk. My diversified, trusted team consists of respected, dedicated, and experienced professionals. As a Project Management Professional from the Project Management Institute, I expect organization and professionalism. As a licensed engineer, who is fully focused on public safety and has transported this obsession to investor safety, I ensure that every investment opportunity meets my stringent criteria for my investors.

Returns

Let's talk about money! I have looked at many different investments and businesses for over a decade. Commercial real estate returns are some of the best returns out there for the least amount of risk. There are different ways to invest, but I am currently helping my investors invest in the down payment of multifamily, NNN, self storage, and light industrial property, which goes toward the equity and makes them an owner. As owners, my investors are eligible for all the tax benefits of owning property without any of the hassle of managing an asset.

Financially, at the time of this writing, my passive commercial real estate investors seek to double their investment in two to five years, which includes full return on their initial investment. They get the benefit of monthly cash flow with a projected cash-on-cash return between three to 12 percent. To compare across all investments, the anticipated internal rate of return is between 14 to 25 percent.

Social Impact

After studying how to end poverty for over a decade and understanding its underlying causes, everything I do now is intentional toward that one goal, even creating wealthier women through multifamily impact investing. Commercial real estate investing has the power to change, at scale, how humans live, and the impact humans have on the environment. If there was one major takeaway that I had while getting my master's, it was that investors and banks hold most of the power when it comes to our built environment. This has a direct impact on environmental, social, and governance (ESG) factors, which are critical to consider for ending poverty.

Environmental

There are many solutions for making an environmental impact in multifamily. As a former LEED AP professional and civil site design engineer, I learned many ways to make buildings and their sites environmentally and economically friendly. Simple solutions include adding more trees, using renewable energy, creating open spaces, and using energy star appliances. Any of these options would allow for both a positive impact on the environment and additional financial gain through tax credits or by reducing expenses. As a water engineer, I care about how drinking water impacts the health of everyone who enters our buildings.

Social

Multifamily assets can be avenues to social impact. They can help provide affordable housing with the benefit of tax credits. In addition, multifamily can be the basis for student housing, senior living, and veteran housing. At a minimum, diversity, equity, and inclusion can be prioritized as part of managing the asset.

Governance

Governance is making positive ethical decisions for all stakeholders, including the investors, the existing community, and society. It is responsible management.

Invest With Me

I am Steph Doblosky, and I help women passively invest in private commercial real estate investments with as little as $50,000 in cash or retirement funds. I partner only with highly trusted and vetted teams so that my investors get the most stable investments for the highest returns from a financial and social impact perspective. I lead with my critical engineering mind and my heart to end poverty and create environmental and social change.

When I'm not investing in multifamily, I use my skills to bring water, sanitation, and hygiene to impoverished people and bring the healthiest drinking water to as many people as I can. This chapter supports the charity Water For People. For more information about this wonderful organization, please visit www.waterforpeople.org.

If you would like to learn more basics about multifamily investing, please feel free to check out my book, *Forget Stocks*, on Amazon. If you wish to invest with me, follow me on social media, speak with me, have me speak at your event, or see what I am up to, go to my website at www.stephdoblosky.com. Together, we will create generational wealth for ourselves, our families, our communities, and our charities.

Steph Doblosky

Steph Doblosky dedicated her life to creating incredible wealth to help end poverty worldwide. She is a licensed professional civil water engineer with a Project Management Professional certification from Project Management Institute, a professional commercial real estate syndicator investor, and a social impact investor, author, speaker, activist, and philanthropist. She is the American Water Works Association Virginia Water For People Chair, a member of Alexandria's Women for Good, and CEO of Zelixer Capital.

Steph cares deeply about every human's right to access clean drinking water and sanitation, which is directly related to several issues wrapped around ending extreme poverty. She is proud of her career as a civil engineer.

She has a Masters of Real Estate Development from the University of Maryland and is an alumnus of Grant Cardone's Real Estate Club and a member of Veena Jetti's Real Estate Club. Steph enjoys bringing people together; she hosts a local meetup group with 36+ members, a local networking group of 45+ members, and a women's commercial real estate networking investing group of 250+ women, where the members encourage one another and work on commercial real estate deals together. She also is the founding hostess of a private, exclusive group of professional women who invest, grow, and give together.

Every Thursday night at 6:30 pm EST, she hosts Ladies Night with Steph Doblosky, featuring a special female commercial real estate guest to discuss their expertise in business or commercial real estate investing, elevating women in her space. She is currently working on a course to help more women invest in private equity to create the generational wealth they need, and the world needs them to have.

Within one year of becoming a syndicator, Steph became a partner on 227 units, specializing in investor relations and capital raising. In her book, Forget Stocks: Billionaire Passive Apartment Investing Secrets, she uncovers how anyone can own multifamily buildings with as little as a $50,000 investment in cash or retirement funds.

Steph is a thought leader in the commercial real estate arena and enjoys encouraging women to elevate themselves to a higher mindset. Steph's vision is to create financially, mentally, and emotionally generationally wealthy women who can finally feel like they are meeting their potential to give back to humanity the way their spirit craves. It's time to stop living in fear and living small. It's time to live in abundance and faith. It's time for global generational impact. That is the freedom that Steph loves achieving within the lives of her clients and her client's investments.

Follow Steph on LinkedIn and Instagram for all things commercial real estate investing, mindset, and water @stephdoblosky and see her website at *www.stephdoblosky.com*. Want passive monthly income that is legally taxed sheltered and backed by commercial real estate assets? Steph's got you. Scan the linktr.ee QR code for your free personal strategy session to learn how to financially get from where you are today to where you want to be. Together we can create the future of your dreams for your family, your community, and your charities.

Chapter 11

WOMEN RISING:

Zero to 2,484 Doors in Four Years How We Got Here

Amber Lackey & Janae Rapps

Janae: Trapped Inside the Lines

One day at work, between patients, my boss sat me down and asked about my life goals. Startled by the question, I gave the standard answer. "I want to be a mom and raise a family." I was 21, had one son, and was pregnant with my second. I was working as a dental assistant for a kind man who had known my dad while they were both in dental school. He saw a version of me that I couldn't imagine and offered me the gift of education. This allowed me the financial ability to attain a DDS degree, just like my late father. My heart was full of gratitude for this opportunity, and I allowed myself the joy of feeling excited about this newfound opportunity. For the rest of the day and all the way home, I started to imagine becoming a dentist and owning my own practice, just like my dad.

"I don't want to be married to someone who makes more than I do!" was the answer I got when I arrived home with my amazing news. I didn't know how to feel. There was so much regret as I turned down the offer, but I resigned to stay between the lines of the path I was on.

Why couldn't I find the confidence I needed then to break free of the path I had been set upon? Maybe it was because I was only a high school graduate, maybe because I was already a mom, or maybe because I was just scared of failure.

Over the next 30 years, I climbed, scraped, and clawed my way from being a dental assistant to a top sales rep for a Fortune 500 company. I worked hard and colored inside the lines to make my way in corporate America and assure my family's security. As a single mom, that's what drove me. But now my boys were growing into men, and I wanted to do something completely on my terms, no matter how far outside the lines.

Amber: Opportunity Disguised as Disaster

I walked into the owner's office nervously, trying to appear confident and put together on my second attempt at my first day of work. I would not acknowledge the pain I was in or the fear I had about taking on this position now. I had wanted it, worked for it, and I was following through.

On the day that was to be my first day, I had taken my dog to the park before work and she ran off into the woods chasing a deer. A hot frantic mess, I called work to tell them I couldn't come in until I found her. They acquiesced, advising me to find my dog, rest, and join them in a few days.

I had walked away from the personal training business I built after 25 years to take this steadier position. I was nervous that the salary I had negotiated would not support me now that I knew I was going to be single. My wife had announced three days earlier that she was leaving. I was heartbroken and exhausted, scared about my future after this recent relationship bomb, and worried that I had undervalued my time in accepting this job.

The owner made it quick: "This is not how you start this job. Now's not the right time." I don't know if I was more upset, mad, or relieved. Overwhelmed, I broke down, realizing I also wasn't sure I could do this now.

Clarity emerged on my drive home via excessive snotty crying, hyperventilation, and a phone-a-friend. I didn't have a job or a wife, but I could now fully admit I was relieved that I didn't have to do this job and sell my time for so much less than I was worth. Big spaces that were just days prior, filled up, were now wide open.

I didn't know what I would do, but I understood that the universe had stepped in and readjusted my trajectory. I felt grateful and loved that such efforts had to be undertaken concurrently by the Universe to move me into this other direction. I surrendered to the knowing that I was meant for something *BIGGER*.

Fast forward two years:

I dragged Janae to a local Real Estate Investing Association meeting, where we were introduced to an educational program about real estate. It painted an amazing future through real estate investing.

This ignited something in me that felt *BIGGER*. I wondered if this was the thing that the Universe had cleared space for. Janae felt her own ignition of independence and opportunity. Her boys were grown, and she was retired and feeling the pull to do something extraordinary.

We could each see it come into focus. This could be the vehicle for those aspirations. Janae was ready. I was hesitant. It was a huge risk, taking on a new venture with ZERO experience, and there was a cost to the mentorship that was a stretch for me. I had a little money left to me when my dad passed away. I remember talking with Janae about this: "I cannot lose this money from my dad; if we do this, *failure is not an option.*" Clarity came for us both. Either of us could have put our money into the stock market, a fund, or some other investment and let somebody else drive the returns. Instead, we decided to bet on ourselves. We trusted ourselves to do right with this investment. We understood what it represented for us, and no one would work harder than us to grow it.

We made the decision. It was done. This was our path; we were going for it. We joined that mentorship and studied our asses off. We started going to real estate networking meetings regularly and got to know people in our area doing real estate successfully. We partnered with lots of different people, continuously worked on our mindset, went to conferences, and continued to grow and learn.

Within four months, we purchased our first house for ~$12K, which was valued at $220K, thanks to our new specialized knowledge! We made some hilarious but ultimately minor mistakes on that first house, and we made a nice little profit off it. Then we kept at it. By the end of that first year in real estate, we had purchased three properties, each for less than $18K, and made our mentorship investment back with an extra 100% on top! That initial investment that once seemed such a stretch started to seem less significant.

Toward the middle of our second year, we invested passively in a colleague's multifamily deal. It became clear very quickly that we didn't understand what we had done. We would watch the investor updates via Zoom and not understand portions of what was said. That set us off on a crusade to learn the language they were using so we could figure out what was going on with this deal. While continuing our single-family investing, we started studying multifamily investing and syndications, which offer opportunities for both active and passive income. And *oh, my goodness*, the tax savings! The ability to provide safe and clean housing for lots of people. The ability to grow our friends' and family's money alongside our own. The ability to scale our business. All these things, coupled with the recession resistance of the asset (everybody needs a place to live!), made us agree that we wanted to move into the multifamily space.

Once again, we went to a multifamily education event where we learned about a multifamily mentorship program. By this time, we knew the drill. We dove into the mentorship, studied our asses off, went to multifamily meetings regularly, started to build connections with people we wanted to work with, and constantly worked on our mindset. We went to conferences and continued to learn and grow. Within three months of being in this mentorship, we teamed up to purchase our first multifamily apartment as co-general partners (active side), and the ball started rolling. By the start of our fourth year in real estate, we added over 1,800 doors to our portfolio. Now, at the start of our fifth year, we have added another 695 doors (across 4 properties) and are on target to purchase three more properties by EOY.

We are so grateful that we decided to bet on ourselves. If we had invested that mentorship money into three of the big stock market indexes, we would have averaged a 56% return over those four-plus years. That would not have changed the quality of our lives. We started with the people we knew and trusted the most, ourselves, and we added mentors, partners and team members to get here. Together we have grown that initial investment over 2,000% in those same four years. That does change the quality of our life – and we are just getting started!

Here are the lessons we've learned that we want to pass on to anybody trying to get into real estate or any new venture.

1. Start with mindset; it is ESSENTIAL to your success. This is a deep and wide topic with concepts ranging from excavating your why to identifying and busting through limiting beliefs, as well as realistic goal setting, visualization, time management, meditation, and more. Janae and I both know, on a cellular level, that we could not have done what we have done without being students of mindset. Two of our biggest mindset resources are Sean Croxton and Tony Robbins.

2. If you can, pay to shorten the learning curve. Our first mentorship changed our lives and put us on the fast track to success (we love you, Big Dogs)! Our second mentorship in multifamily did the same (shout out, Sumrok).

3. Surround yourself with people who are successfully doing what you want to do.

4. Network your ass off. This may sound trite, but it's true. Your network is your net worth.

5. Tell everyone what you do. This might seem sales-y. It's not. If you believe in what you are doing, you are robbing people if you don't tell them about the amazing thing you do and how it could help them.

6. Ask for what you want. Yes, this can be scary. Do it anyway. You miss 100% of the shots you never take.

7. Get out of your comfort zone. Nothing changes there.

8. Do what you say you're going to do. This is more for you than anyone else.

9. Have fun along the way. There is no doubt that there will be days that will bring you to your knees. Say a little prayer while you are down there and get back up and go to the movies. Or play with your kids. Or have an impromptu dance party.

10. Work with people you know, like, and trust.

11. Have a success music playlist (this is our secret weapon). Include songs on this list that will pick you up, inspire you, and, most importantly, songs you will celebrate your wins with when you close the deal, raise that first million, etc. Since you made it all this way in our chapter, we'll share our #1 success song: "Giants" by Walk the Moon. Check it out and see if you are not inspired to go slay Goliath.

In closing, communities of like-minded people and groups have been woven throughout our success. Undoubtedly, we would not be here without the help and support of our chosen circles. We invite you to join our tribe to be inspired and lifted with us as we grow, expand our networks, and invest together. Scan this QR to join our tribe!

THE BEGINNING....

Janae and Amber (aka Jamber) both spent most of their adult lives working for someone else. They made the decision to break out and work for the best boss they could imagine: themselves. In 2019, they started off investing in single-family homes, flipping, wholesaling, and renting. It was so much fun and required *a lot* of work – but the work was for **their own empire.** After two and a half years and roughly 30 homes, the work started to become overwhelming. To continue to grow, they either had to find more hours in the day or figure out how to get paid while they were sleeping. They chose the latter. They invested in an apartment, their first passive multifamily deal. This allowed them to continue their single-family real estate business while making money as they slept. The lightbulb went off. The "aha" happened: They needed to do more of that. They studied multifamily and decided to make the transition to many doors from single doors for the scalability. Along the way, they discovered they had been paying taxes they didn't need to pay. Cue the fireworks, the lights, the marching band, and all. They have since amassed over 2,400 doors to their portfolio and are now on a mission to share these benefits with their friends, family, and fellow investors. They can't wait to show you how to leverage other people's time/expertise/money to passively grow your net worth *and* pay less in taxes!

Chapter 12

A FLICKER OF HOPE:

How a Commercial Saved My Family

Liz Guenthner and Barbie Bowen

A few years ago, we got a call from a family member whom we rarely heard from saying, "Hey, you should invest in this office building. There's no money needed, we just need your personal information, and we will all be rich." Simple, right? The first thing my father did was sign over his personal information and try to talk me and my siblings into signing up as well. I immediately called my financial advisor, who had some questions for this family member, and after she tried to set up a meeting with him, he disappeared. Fast forward about a year later, and my parents seem to have lost most of their savings and added a new mortgage on the family home that had already been paid off. That was my first experience with real estate investing, ironically.

Around that time, Barbie and I were leading a run-of-the-mill life as we followed all the rules and held down a decent little fort. We went to college, got a few degrees, got a couple of jobs, climbed the corporate ladder, traded most of our time for money, rarely had time together, spent almost every dollar each month on whatever, and went on vacation by credit card, making payments when we could. We were making it work but not living below our means or, more importantly, saving toward retirement. I realized we needed to make some changes – but what kind of changes? We were already doing what our parents told us worked for them because eventually, as they said, there would be a pension and a social security check to ride off into the proverbial sunset of our lives.

A couple of years later, I was sitting at home on the couch, sick with the flu, watching who knows what. It was probably a crime show to make myself feel as though it was everyone *else* who was crazy, not me, even though I was doing the same thing repeatedly and expecting something different to happen. Suddenly, I saw a commercial about flipping homes and how real estate can allow you to live on your own terms. Interesting, right? I mean, I saw what investing in real estate did for my folks, but maybe if I could learn how to do it the "right" way, whatever that was, maybe I could make it work for us – and my folks, too. At that moment, Barbie came home with the flu as well, as the flu goes, and I told her about the commercial I saw. She rolled her eyes and said she needed to take some meds and pass out for a bit, so I left her to do just that. Eventually, though, my excitement rubbed off on her, and we went to our first real estate seminar in 2015. The rest is history.

Along the way, and about 120 seminars later (I'm not exaggerating), we learned a few ways to invest in single-family homes, such as wholesaling, holding rentals, flipping, and other creative strategies. However, what really changed our lives and sped up our success was multifamily investing, mainly in apartments, and we now realize the true power of scaling the number of doors you own. Currently, we are partners in almost 700 doors and hope to continue scaling our business while helping others invest as well. But before we could do all this, we had to get our minds right. When things would get tough, as life sometimes does, we would tell ourselves, "Hey, we are two smart women; we can make this work."

Typically, when you want to learn something new that's challenging, you react in different ways. You can put more effort in and trudge through or shy away from the struggle to find an easier path. There were times when we wanted to give up and just work our W2 jobs, taking the weekends off to over-consume things – all the things. Yet when you learn that there is another system that few people know about but that's available to everyone, one that offers financial freedom and more time to focus on your passions, things shift in your mind, body, and spirit; a complete shift of actions and habits arise based on a new knowing and awareness of potential. When things were stressful in the beginning, we needed a mantra to repeat, to silence the crazy monkey thoughts of self-doubt. We needed to recenter ourselves and remember the catalyst of this journey. We needed to find our "why." Why were we working our regular jobs AND starting another one? Why were we spending all this money on more education when we already had degrees? We went through an exercise to really identify where we came from and where we were going. It was at that point that we realized that it made perfect sense that we were two smart women making it work at all costs because we came from two amazing women who made it work at all costs: our mothers.

My mom's name is Lydia Guenthner (maiden name Vasquez), and she was born and raised in a small town in Mexico called Piedras Negras. My grandfather was a carpenter and would ride his bike across the border into Texas, a few miles each way, to make money for the family, and my grandmother would cook and clean for families in the area. Even though she had very few belongings as a child, my mother felt rich with familial ties since many generations lived in a cluster on the same block. When she was around the age of 10, her family moved to Eagle Pass, Texas, and settled down away from the cluster to become migrant workers, traveling up and down the West Coast to pick fruit and vegetables for farmers.

Barbie and I recently took an RV trip up the same coast, and I often thought about her experiences working in the hot sun and sleeping in the temporary dirt-floored shelters the farmers provided for the families working their land. I would ask her questions like, "Didn't you feel poor in those days, Mom?" She answered me with, "Not at all, we didn't know what we didn't have, and we always had plenty of food around us all the time in the fields. You get hungry, you pick something, and you eat it. Onions, right from the dirt, are so sweet and delicious. Plus, our whole family was together, and we felt safe."

At a certain age, my mom was given the choice to work with the family or go to school, so she chose school in search of a different path. I'm thankful that she shared her experiences with me and still reminds me how important education is in changing your path. She taught me what it means to "work hard;" my complaints as a teenager were met with comments like, "Oh, you think studying for this test is hard?" or, "You think your little sister is difficult?" and, "Let me tell you about how hard I worked just to get to school." Those types of stories will snap you back to reality and quickly put things into perspective. My mom's drive and work ethic are instilled in me to better myself every day and, eventually, take care of her in return and thank her for her efforts.

Barbie's mom's name is Mary Ellen, or Meme if you're a friend, and she was born in Wisconsin into a farming family of English and German descent. After a divorce in the family, Meme was a single parent and worked as a real estate agent in Austin, Texas. It's amazing to see the yellowed marketing materials we have with her picture on them from the 1980s, where she highlighted the benefits of owning a home while interest rates floated around 18%. Oh, the '80s – I hope we never see the likes of you again.

As Barbie entered her teens, Meme would buy a house and make updates to improve it, only to sell for a profit and do it all over again. Since she didn't understand her mom's entrepreneurial efforts, Barbie found it difficult to see the value of uprooting the family in the name of an old home that needed work. Looking back, she now understands what her mom was doing to stay ahead of the curve, but back then, moving around was not the ideal way to maintain friendships. Ironically, Meme would tell Barbie to never consider real estate as a career path since the ups and downs were too volatile, and she should try something more stable. In 2016, we lost Barbie's mom to complications from Alzheimer's, and we often wonder what her stance would be now, watching what we've been able to accomplish in the volatile industry of real estate. Meme's tenacity to keep moving forward and make something more out of something less is what drives Barbie to be the best real estate agent in Austin and the best syndicator for her multifamily investors. Honoring her mother's legacy pushes her to help others turn their something less into something more.

What was once confusing, frustrating, and even financially painful for my parents is the tool we use to help ensure they can retire gracefully. What was once a tumultuous, uncertain career for a single mom making it work at all costs is the instrument we use to make our future more clear and secure. Our company is called BE Property Investors. The "B" is for Barbie, and the "E" is for Elizabeth (but only the nuns in private school called me that). As time has passed, the micro view of our namesakes has transformed into a macro one. We realize what investing in real estate can do for all families and communities, and now we want everyone else to "BE" property investors and be prosperous. Herein lies our "why": We believe everyone should not only retire gracefully to spend time with family but also create legacy wealth for the next generations and, ultimately, give back to our communities. Beyond that, we improve properties to provide better housing for families while creating jobs in different markets. It's a full circle of prosperity.

In writing this book, Barbie and I thought about what we should share to help others on their journey. Maybe we should mention knowing and trusting the team you invest with – the opposite of what my parents did in their first real estate deal. Maybe we should talk about skipping single-family investing and going straight into multifamily, though we learned a lot from both strategies and wouldn't change a thing. Maybe we should mention letting go of fear so that you can get in front of people to network openly and honestly about opportunities you believe in. We are both introverts, so this is a constant battle, but our "why" is bigger than any fear.

After some consideration, we've realized the most important thing that you need on this journey toward success. It's not what you know, it's not how you apply what you know, and it's not even who you know, even though all these things are extremely important in this game. It comes down to knowing yourself and identifying your "why." See, I can tell you the details of the "what" and the "how" that led to some of our successes, and you can apply them to your journey. But when things get beyond stressful, if there's nothing driving or grounding you, most likely revert and return to the comfort of your couch, binge-watching your crime show to feel less crazy than other people, like I used to. Once you realize and zero in on your "why," you'll have found the secret sauce that will push you forward. No one else can identify or activate that but you. The other stuff can be learned, practiced, managed, and improved. I truly believe everyone can learn anything and has the potential to be great at something. It's just a matter of focusing your energy on a goal, fueled by the reason that made you get off the couch in the first place. You're a smart woman (or man), and you can make this work, I'm sure. But make it work...why? Talk soon.

Liz Guenthner and Barbie Bowen

Liz Guenthner and Barbie Bowen currently live in Austin, Texas, along with the best dog-in-training, Lucy. After attending college together at the University of Texas, they chose different career paths before finding real estate investing in 2015. Liz has a bachelor's in fine arts, an MBA in entrepreneurial studies, and works as a software developer. Barbie has a bachelor's in kinesiology and transitioned from a career in business operations to full-time real estate. Together, they manage single-family properties, actively syndicate multifamily deals, and own over 680 doors in Texas, Georgia, and Florida. In order to stay connected and up to date on market trends, they maintain memberships with multiple investing groups and attend seminars and meetups around the nation. Aside from real estate investing, their passions include traveling to beautiful beach towns like Isla Mujeres, Mexico, listening to live music at local festivals, and walking Lucy along the lake in downtown Austin. When they reach financial freedom, Barbie looks forward to creating a senior pup sanctuary in the beautiful Texas Hill Country, and Liz plans to continue writing and illustrating children's books. In the end, it's all about having time to do what you love while giving back to those you love. https://bepropertyinvestors.com

Chapter 13

TO BE EMPOWERED:
The Mindset. The Struggle. The Journey.

Karen Singh

A Brooklyn girl from East New York (ENY) in the 1970s couldn't have imagined what life was about to unfold. My father's murder in late 1984 would change our family's life forever. At the time, my twin brother and I were twelve years old, and my younger brother was eleven. My mother was a factory worker on food stamps with very little spoken English. Only now can I understand and somehow feel all that she must have felt and gone through to keep us shielded from the uncertainties of raising three kids as a single mom in the streets of ENY. She eventually packed and moved us to her country, Cartagena, Colombia.

Even though we had visited a few times before, living in a third-world country was a whole different ball game. My brothers and I had a year of homeschooling because schools in Cartagena after 6th grade were private. After finally getting settled into our surroundings, my mom later that year, in 1986, said we were moving to Puerto Rico. My brothers and I felt like we just wanted to die. At the time, we couldn't understand that my mother could not afford to stay in this country as she could not afford to pay for private schooling for her three kids and was not able to find a well-paid job.

I was fourteen years old when we moved to a country we knew nothing about, as our father never really talked about or introduced Puerto Rico to us other than through music. It took us the summer and first year of junior high school to fit in. I can't speak for my brothers, but over the years, I felt like it was home; I learned to love the island and made great friendships.

In 1996, I finished my bachelor's degree in psychology and in 2001 master's degree in counseling while working in the restaurant industry. In 2004 I married, moved to Miami, and after three months, became pregnant and had my daughter at the age of thirty–two. I worked in healthcare management as an operations manager overseeing multiple healthcare centers, one of the best skill set learning experiences. My now ex-husband and I purchased our first home in 2006. In 2013, I purchased my first investment property, a single-family home in Liberty City in Miami, with inheritance money. My mother and husband at the time insisted I was crazy, but I knew real estate was a sure way to go. Why, may you ask? Well, I'll tell you. The property values in my old neighborhood in Brooklyn, New York, had increased over the years. In the Miami area in 2013, SFHs were being sold under value due to the crash of 2008. I did not have to be in real estate to know that property values would increase, as I had seen with my own eyes throughout my life in New York, Colombia, Puerto Rico, and Miami how the value of properties decreased and later increased by two to three times their original worth.

In 2021, I sold the property and made a profit of $260,000. I know, I know, I should not have sold it. In prior years, I tried to purchase another property, but after my divorce, my credit went to shit, and the banks would not approve me. All the while, Grant

Cardone was making a killing in real estate in my backyard, but I did not know he existed.

Unfortunately, I didn't have the right people around me to steer me in the right direction. Also, to my own detriment, I believed million-dollar properties were above my status. If I had known how to leverage other people's money and the right ways to approach banks, these would have been only a few of the paths I could have taken.

Today, at fifty years of age, I am remarried to a Trinidadian, have an eighteen-year-old daughter and seven-year-old son, and my life has taken another turn. Real estate has been evolving faster than I have, but there is still time to have a piece of that brick. In February 2023, my husband and I began to work with a real estate broker looking for SFHs and duplexes, and after walking a few, we realized the investment was far greater than the return and just didn't feel like enough. I began on a journey to learn more about multifamily investments, became a member of a few real estate groups on Facebook for free, and got hooked.

My personal connection to the groups was missing, but I continued learning and viewing videos. Then I came across a Grant Cardone video and was intrigued by the short man. I began to watch but wasn't crazy about the presentation. It felt fake. He said it was live, but it was a recording, and he was selling books and gear. His face was so far away from the camera, and I remember he had a sidekick named Jarrod. I moved on from the video, and that's when all hell broke loose. The calls started coming in from GC's team. I think I hung up about twenty times; what a pain in the ass those calls were.

About two weeks after viewing the GC video, I was leaving the gym when my phone rang. I answered the call, and there it was: a GC sales call. I told the guy he had two minutes to tell me what he was selling and how his bothering me was going to change my mind. After a track of questions, the poor guy handed the call to another person. He said his name was Ben, and I'll never forget that call.

Ben sounded honest, made me laugh, and answered every question with flying colors. After about a 30-minute call, I arrived home. He waited for me to access my credit card, and I paid my $500 ticket for the March 2023 RE summit in Aventura. It was an amazing summit, resulting in a mindset change. In the last two minutes before the summit was over that Sunday, Grant said, "You will go home, open the door to your house, and life will happen. You'll keep trying to play this real estate game by yourself, and you will go back to your life." At that moment, with tears rolling down my cheeks and my soul telling me, *that's you, woman,* I knew he was right. Like I mentioned earlier, with the wrong broker looking at the wrong properties, doing it myself (well, with my hubby, too) simply wasn't going to work.

The only thing I was doing right was the daily exercises that kept me moving forward. I got up from my chair and joined the Real Estate Club, and ten weeks later, my life began transitioning as I connected the dots and put the pieces of my puzzle together. Finally, I found the connection.

What is the first shift for a beginner entering into the multifamily real estate industry?

Mindset: I accepted part of my growth in life before today was due to my perseverance and the influence of mentors who may not even have been aware of their impact. My family in Colombia, including uncles and cousins who were doctors, dentists, engineers, architects, and other professionals or aspiring professionals in university, whom served as examples to me. At 13 years of age, I told myself I could be a professional too. Today, I accept that even as a professional, one's mindset is still limiting if you're not around the right people. The right people are those who are wealthy, not just in finances but also in mindset. Today I know that those with a title, a couple of dollars in the bank, a nice house, and a car are still broke; many professionals have negative debt and lack the financial plan to become wealthy with positive debt instead.

Elevated mindset: Get out of your head. What is your why? You will hear this more than you can imagine. Stop and internalize your why, as this journey will be a new way of life for you and your family. It is not for the weak or absent-minded. Use your confidence, not your ego. If you don't have confidence, it will grow.

When I decided to leave the corporate world of healthcare and work for myself, I had all the confidence in the world until I lost it. I was a strong, go-forward kind of woman, and I lost myself. Uncertainty, fear, feelings of frustration with myself and not having the right people around caused my feelings of purpose to suddenly become dark, and I could not see my path anymore. If you are afraid, it's okay. That's good. Fear will turn into confidence and strength, and a broken mindset will give you urgency.

Your improved mindset is your new way of life. You will learn to be comfortable when you put into practice the process of MF real estate.

1. Read books on MF structure, how to raise capital, what a fund is, and how it benefits you and your investors.
2. In the realm of business, a mind-blowing realization occurred

for me during GC sales training: the understanding that my thoughts ultimately shape my actions, and these actions, in turn, define my success. If I sell the customer based on what I think instead of the best 10X offer, then that is what I will get.

3. Exercise – I can't stress this enough. Having an exercise routine will provide a healthy, strong mindset, physical endurance, and energy. The weakness and fear will begin to dissolve. Your body is your throne; without it, none of this is possible.

4. Alcohol is a Debbie Downer. I'll be transparent; that's what this chapter is about. Drinking was my stress reliever; it was my friend, as crazy as it reads. Until it wasn't. Drinking stopped being my friend, stopped being fun, and that Karen is now gone. Don't get it twisted, I'll have a drink now and then, but that person is no longer here. See, the Almighty told me a while ago that my time was near, and this Karen was to be no more. You see, if your life must change, **you** need to make the change, or the transition will not occur or fail to be permanent.

Your Why: That was not easy for me. My purpose? To really deep dive, I realized my why were my children, my family. What example was I really setting for them? Elevating my mindset, my actions, and my persona would hopefully make a difference in theirs as well. My purpose in life has always been a part of my personality helping those whom could not help themselves not realizing that's part of my why. As life has also shown me the horrors via movies and/or other people's stories of human trafficking. I've prayed and have in my heart the pain and concern as a mother every day that my children are safe and vigilant of the realities around them. It is difficult for me to know how I can be of service to this problem in our world. but open to the universe and ready when my time comes. The feeling of responsibility to help them is very real. This education system and government do not empower our children with the necessary tools to be successful. Its a must to unite with like-minded people to provide our children with safer tomorrows.

Financial Planning- What is your financial goal (not your budget)? What is that uncomfortable dollar amount you want to reach? Remember, $1,000,000 may seem like a lot, but think about it: after taxes, you're left with about $700,000. The average cost of an SFH is $500,000. Go beyond. Until recently, I could not even fathom a number over a million. We have been crippled by society. Don't be afraid to aspire to this number (over a million). If you don't, you will not work hard enough to get there. Grant says money is an imaginary number; we make it up. At first, I could not understand his concept. I thought he was out of his mind. After lots of training, I see it. You will never be able to internalize it right away. It's mind-blowing when you do.

My suggested daily schedule- Exercise routine. Cardone University or your personal training course. UW training. A day or two out of the week to search deals, walk properties, and build relationships with brokers. Zoom training, webinars with guest speakers (golden nuggets every time), networking, live and/or virtual events, and boot camps. If you're a W-2 and/or growing your business 10X, additional marketing/sales training. I usually start my day at 6:00 am. That's starting to feel like it's too late. Be uncomfortable with yourself. You will succeed. Have fun on the journey. I am.

Family and Friends- When you first enter the MF environment, you can't really conceptualize what it takes to be in this world. If you're not willing to change the way you act, think, and work, this life will be very heavy on you and will not last. It is not enough to train or purchase a property. The change is a daily routine; it's real, and you will feel it unfold every day. My family was on board with my new routine until time with them was affected – my friends as well. The positive outcome, if you stick to your guns and continue, is that your family and real friends will be your top supporters.

I see my husband and kids becoming more understanding and supportive. It gives me a sense of motivation and enhances my confidence and courage to continue. If my husband sees me on the sofa for over 20 minutes, he says, "Aren't you supposed to be doing something more productive?" I just smile, get up from my break, and continue. Don't get me wrong, I still wash clothes, clean the house (when it looks like a hurricane came through), and care for my children and my mother, but I cook less. LOL!

Underwriting- Learn to underwrite in two minutes, including how to do a deep underwrite. Grant tells us to use the napkin underwriting approach, incorporating the calculation of interest and principal into those two minutes. Initially, I made the mistake of not doing this, and other seniors advised me, "No, Karen, you need to learn deep underwriting before you pitch a deal." I began to learn, and by the way, it takes a lot of time and practice. I began to feel anxious because looking for deals and speaking to brokers was taking a backseat. I also paid to learn. Bibi, a beautiful person, must have felt my pain when I requested help in the group. She replied, "Karen, I'll help you for free."

Our schedules conflicted, and we never could make it happen, but thank you, Bibi, for reaching out. I later found a person whom I paid through a member of the GC club. Jon Sedoti, you're the best. In one of our GC Club weekly calls, Grant said, "If you use most of your time deep underwriting a deal, you'll miss out on the deal. You see, a deep dive UW is completed if the two-minute UW makes sense, but not before."

Why go through all that work and time only to find out it's not a good deal? You see, you need to underwrite at least 25-50 deals to get one or two. The golden nugget I learned that made the pressure go away: Learning deep underwriting is important when the deal makes sense. Even if you're not doing the UW on your deals, it's important to know all aspects. Don't be in the dark because people can take advantage of you. We are all human, after all.

Building Relationships? One of the most uncomfortable and time-consuming processes is learning to speak on stages. You'll need a speech. Stages with Pete Vargas is excellent. Speaking engagements are the most humbling, exciting, and incredible experiences in my new life. They allow me to build relationships with like-minded investors who are seniors in this lifestyle and to adjust to my new skin. In my experience, the toughest crowd has been the women. We women are a different breed. The Almighty made us from birth to be tough as bricks. To be around accomplished, empowered women can be an uncomfortable feeling but also the most empowering.

Women, as a team, are the most powerful strength on this earth. As a woman who has full experience of struggle, I know we are an undeniable force. We are still dominated by men, but in the MF space, I've not felt at any point that men have disrespected or treated me any less because I'm a woman.

Be active in building relationships and learn to be uncomfortable with yourself. The more uncomfortable you are with yourself, the more you're empowered to learn and practice urgency in every step you take. Learn to build relationships with brokers and potential investors. This piece is one of the most difficult because transparency is key. "Don't tell me, show me" is good advice to follow. Be present.

Go to virtual summits and be present at MF RE events. You will begin to see many familiar faces, and conversations will begin to strengthen. Next thing you know, you'll be a part of a deal or have investors for one of your deals. My time is coming soon; I can smell it. Why? I am present, learning, working, and using my time to benefit myself and my family. The benefits of owning 30-plus units provide the capability to pay a management company without the cost hurting the return on investment.

The Pitch. It's all in the pitch. My first pitch to the Real Estate Club was an amazing experience. To role-play with Grant Cardone himself and pitch to a broad group of beginners and multi-millionaires is an opportunity not too many people can experience. To pitch to potential investors, be knowledgeable of your deal. Know the purchase price, number of units, equity, debt, and, most of all, why the property is being sold. You must also know the cash on cash and the Net Operating Income (NOI). Be honest and transparent no matter how difficult or embarrassed you may feel. I'm currently in the middle of the awkwardness and nerves that come while you're getting the hang of pitching. Just get through it; it's all about practicing and doing the work.

To be part of a Syndication. Learn how to structure a deal, which includes gaining knowledge of the terms LP, GP, and key person. Learn what syndication is and the value of each person in that group. My value is that I'm great with communication, outgoing, and not afraid to be around or speak to others. My skills from running medical clinics provide me the advantageous knowledge of asset management and building maintenance. Syndication will come in time. The key is to learn to love this game. If you don't love it, don't do it.

The MF journey – and I've said this before – is a new way of life, a new way of thinking, speaking, and asking questions. No one will hold your hand. Building personal connections and establishing relationships with syndication individuals is not only valuable but provides an opportunity for mutual vetting. This holds true for any syndication.

My speech pattern is evolving. Now that my mindset has elevated, I have two-minute and 15-minute scripts to promote my business, speak to brokers, and attract potential investors. This change did not happen overnight, but in 10 weeks, my manner of speaking did adjust. My words are now shorter and to the point. I don't have unnecessary conversations. Silence is also becoming familiar.

If you embark on this journey, your wake-up time will be earlier. Mark my words. To start, make GC's five priorities in real estate your everyday mantra: deals, debt, cash/equity, network, and confidence. If you're interested in how my journey pans out, you'll have to wait for the next chapter. It will be juicy! Let's get on this journey together. Catch up; I'm not slowing down.

Karen Singh., BS, M.ed

In 2018 started as an entrepreneur, owning and operating a travel business as Franchisee, Namaste Escapes, LLC. The success I have achieved does not defy who I am, rather the journey to achieve those successes. My diverse background in restaurant, healthcare, and travel has empowered me to take leadership roles to a different level. Driving Excellence and Empowering Teams, Personal Growth and Community Engagement. A journey defined by exceptional adaptability, My ability to innovate, inspire teams, and navigate diverse industries showcases my unwavering commitment to success. I've strived to be a woman that defies society, that defies the norms of tradition, where a woman is taught to surrender and become content. I'm passionate and love what I do, commit and conquer. As I continue my journey in the Multi Family Real Estate Industry as a Passive/Active Investor contributing to my community. The impact of a team and dedication will undoubtedly leave a lasting legacy. Committed with people that represent and work for freedom. Relentless.

To reach me click below:

enykaren624@gmail.com

www.namasteescapes.com

karen.singh@cruiseplanners.com

Chapter 14

FROM VETERAN TO MULTIFAMILY INVESTOR:
The Journey Toward Wealth Creation

Shirley Baez

The idea of compound interest, saving, and investing has always interested me since I was young. You see, I had a tough childhood that revolved around a scarcity mindset. I witnessed the struggles and hardships of both my parents, one who never wanted to work and the other who worked too hard but barely made ends meet. They always thought there was never enough of anything. Growing up in scarcity taught me the value of money and the importance of financial literacy.

It wasn't until I joined the military that I had the opportunity to acquire a paycheck and explore different possibilities for investing my money. I was able to invest the traditional way (mutual funds, CDs, ETFs, etc.) The conventional method of investing helped create a good baseline of savings, but toward the end of my 20-year career in the military, I knew there had to be more to now build on what I already had. It was time to create generational wealth through tangible assets.

It was exciting the way I began this journey into multifamily. As I was getting ready to retire from the military, I wanted to move and sell my home in NC to move to Tampa, Florida. I was so eager to sell and take the profits. My stepmother at the time insisted that

I shouldn't, and I couldn't understand why she was hell-bent on me not selling. You see, as I was thinking of short-term gains, she was thinking of long-term strategic use of the equity for bigger projects and investments.

I decided to get out of my own self-limitations and went ahead, kept the NC property, rented it, and subsequently conducted a "cash out refi" where I could leverage the equity of my home to invest in anything I wanted. This was my opportunity; I invested some of the money in a luxury beach property in Cap Cana, Dominican Republic, which I am turning into a short-term rental.

Woah! What a leap of faith! I can't thank my stepmother enough for pushing me to think bigger. Now that I had gotten my feet wet renting out my home and investing in a short-term rental, I was ready to re-challenge myself. I was curious to learn what it would look like to invest in Apartments and Multifamily. This is an arena I did not know how to navigate because I thought that I needed a lot of money, experience, and connections to get into the real estate/multifamily investing space. I was intimidated by the complexity and risk of the business.

One day, I stumbled upon a podcast that changed my perspective. *Bigger Pockets* features interviews with successful real estate investors who share their stories, strategies, and tips. I had also read the book authored by Robert Kiyosaki called *Rich Dad, Poor Dad* (some call it "The Purple Bible"). Finally, I came across Grant Cardone through the App Clubhouse. I attended his Business Bootcamp, which ultimately led me to attend his Real Estate Summit; the rest was history.

I learned that multifamily investing is one of the most lucrative and scalable ways to create passive income and long-term wealth. I also learned that there are many ways to finance, analyze, and operate multifamily properties without doing everything alone.

I decided to begin this multifamily journey by listening to more podcasts, reading books, and joining online communities related to multifamily investing. I also attended local meetups and events where I met other like-minded investors and professionals. I realized there is a whole world of opportunities and resources for anyone wanting to learn and act. Through these events, I met two seasoned investors with a track record of finding and managing profitable properties. After vetting them, I decided to take the plunge and use the other portion of my cash-out refi to invest in my first multifamily deal as a limited partner (LP).

I am enjoying the benefits of multifamily investing. I receive checks from the property's cash flow, which cover some of my living expenses and allow me to save to reinvest in more deals. I also benefit from the property's appreciation, tax advantages, and equity growth, which increase my net worth and long-term wealth, and this is just the beginning. I am proud to be a part of a community of investors who positively impact the lives of their tenants, partners, and themselves.

Creating passive income by investing in cash flow assets that never depreciate has changed my life completely. Aside from my rental property in NC and the development of my beach property in the Caribbean, I am planning to rent out my current home so that I can use my Veterans Assistance home loan (VA loan) to purchase a small multifamily, where I can live in one of the apartments while renting out the others. What I love about the VA loan is that it is offers a guaranteed loan with zero down to all active-duty military members and veterans.

I love this multifamily space because you can get as creative as possible in building several passive income streams. My tenacity in focusing on my goal led me to an opportunity of joining a team as a General Partner (GP). This opportunity resulted from showing my value, network development, and eagerness to give and learn. As a result, being on the team has taught me how to find deals, underwrite and evaluate deals, raise capital, negotiate contracts, manage assets, and oversee daily operations.

We are aiming to purchase our first 30-40-unit apartment building in a growing market with strong cash flow and upside potential. We also plan to hire a professional property management company to handle the day-to-day operations. Multifamily, for me, is so much fun and fulfilling because I am providing a decent place to live for others and implementing value-add strategies such as improving the curb appeal, renovating the units, and providing other amenities to elevate the quality of life for our future tenants.

I am grateful that I learned about multifamily investing and acted. It has been one of the best decisions of my life. I am excited to continue learning, growing, and investing in more multifamily properties in the future. As a woman, it is important for me to break the glass ceiling in a heavily male-dominated industry.

Women have long been marginalized and excluded from the lucrative field of real estate investment, especially in the commercial sector. Despite their potential and interest, women face many barriers and challenges that prevent them from entering and succeeding in this industry. These challenges include misrepresentation and a lack of mentorship, funding, education, and confidence that they can do it.

That's why I must educate women about alternative investments, such as multifamily investments, so they can create generational wealth and not settle for the status quo,

Ladies, here are the ten principles that I live by when I am working on a goal, specifically on my multifamily journey:

1. **Start with your "why":** Write down your goals and purpose for wanting to break into this space. Find out your motivations and vision for why you want to invest in multifamily real estate. Identifying your goals will help you stay focused, overcome challenges, and find your niche.

2. **Educate yourself:** Learn as much as you can about multifamily. Read books, listen to podcasts, join online communities, and attend real estate events.

3. **Understanding different types of real estate investing:** There are many ways to invest in real estate, such as buying and holding rental properties, flipping houses, wholesaling properties, investing in commercial real estate, or investing in real estate investment trusts (REITs). Each type has its own advantages, disadvantages, risks, and rewards. You should learn the pros and cons of each and choose which area will most likely get you to your goals.

4. **Build your network:** Connect with other like-minded individuals who are on the same journey or beyond and are crushing it. Network with brokers, lenders, and anyone who can assist you on your path and provide you opportunities and resources.

5. **Seek mentorship and coaching.** Find someone who has achieved what you want and learn from their experience and advice. A mentor or coach can help you avoid common pitfalls, accelerate your learning curve, and expand your network.

6. **Join a women-focused group or platform.** There are many groups and platforms that cater to women investors and professionals in the multifamily space. These can provide support, inspiration, education, and opportunities to connect and collaborate with other women.

7. **Act and learn from mistakes:** Don't let analysis paralysis stagnate you from your goals; take the leap of faith and start small and build your way up. Also, you should be prepared to face challenges and setbacks along the way but don't let those stagnate you. Keep striving towards your goals.

8. **Give without expecting anything in return:** As you learn the ropes and make connections, you will also encounter many opportunities to demonstrate your value through helping others. The best way to gain trust from a potential group or partner is to act in good will and share your knowledge and skills without expectations. Trust me, it will be the biggest return on investment ever.

9. **Be Confident:** Believe in yourself and your abilities. Be fearless, and don't let stereotypes or biases discourage or limit your highest potential. Show that you can bring value; don't be afraid to show your knowledge and skills.

10. **Celebrate your wins, give back, and share your story.** Don't be afraid to celebrate your achievements and share your journey with others. This will help you build your credibility,

confidence, and brand. It can also inspire and empower other women to follow in your footsteps.

Although there are challenges, they are easy to overcome. I want to bring awareness, advocacy, education, and support so that women can overcome self-imposed barriers and believe they can achieve their goals in this space. As women, we have proven that we are resilient, go-getters, resourceful, and successful in many other fields, and there is no reason why we cannot do the same in the multifamily space. As more women enter and excel in this industry, they will create a positive impact on themselves, their families, communities, and society.

Real estate investing is one of the most powerful ways to create wealth and achieve financial independence. That is why women need to break into real estate investing and claim their share of the opportunities and benefits. Women can generate passive income, build equity, enjoy tax advantages, and diversify their portfolios by investing in real estate, and doing so will empower them to take control of their finances, pursue their passions, and live their dreams.

I vowed to do better for myself and my future family. For me, right now, financial freedom is not a luxury; it is a necessity. It is the foundation of my independence, my security, and my happiness. I learned how to budget, save, and invest my money wisely in my early years. I educated myself on personal finance and wealth creation principles and practices, and I developed a mindset of abundance and opportunity rather than scarcity and limitation so that I can be free to live my best life.

Ladies, see your future self being financially independent because it is the key to unlocking your full potential to live your best life. You deserve to have financial freedom; you deserve to enjoy all the great things that life can bring, and you know what? You have the power to achieve it! Don't let anyone or anything hold you back from pursuing your dreams. You are strong, smart, and capable. You are a woman who can do anything.

Shirley Baez

Shirley Baez is a retired Army Special Operations veteran with 20 years of service. She is a mentor and coach who inspires hundreds of people to discover and unleash their true greatness. She is the founder and CEO of the LeadHERship Academy, a company that focuses on helping women break through self-imposed barriers so they can become the confident, decisive, creative, and influential leaders they are meant to be in their personal and professional lives.

Shirley is a speaker and the author of the book *Lead Your Ship, unlock your true self and Captain your ship like a boss.*

She is also a co-author of the Amazon bestseller series *Powerful Female Immigrant.* She is an active multifamily, vacation rentals, and single-family investor with over 170 apartment units in her portfolio. Through her coaching, she shares her passion for helping people and gives them the tools they need to succeed and lead their ship in all aspects of life.

Chapter 15

MULTIFAMILY UDERWRITING:

3 Most Important Things to Consider

Anastasia Makarska

Thank you for coming to say 'hi' to me as a reader. I feel humbled that you are investing your valuable time to learn how I can help you. You will be glad you read this chapter, as I believe you will find a plethora of helpful information for your life and business.

When my ex-husband, small child, and I first came to the United States, we were both highly educated (with Master's degrees in Physics). However, we had very little money and no jobs. We had left everything behind in our home country, Ukraine, in search of a better life, but the harsh reality of our situation quickly set in. Struggling in a cold New Jersey winter, unable to speak English and without any acquaintances in this new country, we realized that we needed to find our own place to live and support ourselves.

Finding jobs was a difficult task for us as we had limited English skills and no connections in the community. We spent weeks searching, but despite our efforts, we often went to bed hungry. To make matters worse, we didn't even have a proper bed for seven years, and our child, who was under five years old, didn't have a single toy for the first two years. One day, we were down to our last few dollars and knew we had to do something drastic. So, we put our pride aside and went to a local food bank, where we were given bags of groceries to take home. It was a humbling experience, but it provided us with the sustenance we needed to keep going. Although it was a tough time, it taught me the importance of perseverance and the value of community support.

Fast forward to my PhD studies in Physics at Georgia Institute of Technology in Atlanta, Georgia, and my enjoyable time at Eastern Virginia Medical School in Norfolk, where I was honored with a prestigious Director's Award. After working for a decade in surgery (my last job title was Neurophysiologist), I decided to venture into real estate investing on a part-time basis. Like many others, I started by investing in single-family homes (SFH) and was able to replace my medical income with cash flow fairly quickly. Despite having no prior knowledge of construction, I simultaneously managed several renovation projects. I'm excited to share with you exactly how I accomplished this feat. You can do the same if you're committed to the process. Simply follow the link below to download my free guide, 'How to Quickly Replace Your Job Income with Cash Flow from SFH Rentals'.

I was intrigued by the success of my rental portfolio, and with my natural entrepreneurial spirit (having previously supervised over 100 people and managed a successful business in Ukraine), I became driven to achieve more. I went on to establish and succeed with multiple companies, becoming practically unstoppable. If I were to summarize my path to success in five words, it would be: 'Being there before being there.' Or, "**BE** there before you **be** there". I will explain it later. I studied highly successful people, attuned my emotional state to what they would feel, and used that energy to take massive action and calculated risks, and being patient. I expected the best but was prepared for any obstacles, like carrying an umbrella even on a sunny day. The days of my state of being are always sunny!

I have established several real estate verticals over time, including founding development and construction companies that have worked on projects ranging from single-family home remodeling with zen-build.com to large-scale, multi-story commercial enterprise. I also established a real estate brokerage that helps to sponsor licensed real estate agents-investors. My assisted living brand AbbeCareHomes.com is doing well, and for those interested in assisted living investing or operations, I will soon be releasing training on how to make $10,000 of net income per month, per home. Large deals require larger down payments, so I have another vertical that raises capital for such deals, and yet another that provides property management.

Naturally, my next move was to organize syndications and take on large multifamily deals. I remember attending a Grant Cardone real estate summit and getting so excited about underwriting multifamily properties that I found myself explaining the process to others in a hotel lobby until 2 o'clock in the morning! From that point on, I have underwritten numerous deals with meticulous attention to detail, crunching numbers until they appear in my pro-forma like magic spells.

Multifamily underwriting might sound like a complex and intimidating term, but fear not, my dear reader, for I am here to break it down for you. Think of it as a process of evaluating the financial feasibility (likelihood or probability of succeeding) of investing in a property that houses multiple families, like a fancy apartment complex. And if you want to dive deeper into the nitty-gritty details, I've got you covered in my upcoming book, "Underwriting Multifamily on a Napkin, the Grant Cardone Math Explained.

There are three most important things to consider in every multifamily deal underwriting.

1. Cash flow analysis:

Cash flow analysis is a crucial aspect of multifamily underwriting, as it provides insight into the property's ability to generate income and produce a return on investment. In essence, cash flow analysis involves examining the property's income and expenses to determine the net operating income (NOI). NOI is calculated by subtracting operating expenses from the property's gross income. This figure provides a more accurate representation of the property's income-generating potential as it accounts for expenses such as property taxes, insurance, and maintenance costs.

To calculate cash flow, NOI is then used to subtract debt service, or mortgage payments, and any other financing costs. The resulting figure represents the property's cash flow, or the amount of money made by the property after all expenses have been accounted for. This number is a key indicator of the property's investment potential, as it shows whether the property can generate enough income to cover its expenses and provide a return on investment.

When conducting cash flow analysis, we will often examine historical financial data as well as projected income and expenses. Historical data provides insights into the property's past performance and can help us identify trends and potential risks. Projected income and expenses, on the other hand, provide insight into the property's future performance and can help us make informed investment decisions.

Cash flow analysis can also be used to evaluate the potential impact of different investment scenarios. For example, we may analyze the effects of increasing rents, reducing expenses, or implementing a capital improvement plan. By examining the impact of different scenarios on cash flow, we can make more informed investment decisions and identify strategies to maximize the property's value.

2. Market analysis:

Conducting a thorough market analysis is crucial when underwriting a multifamily property. This involves examining demographic trends, economic indicators, supply and demand dynamics, and other factors that can impact the property's value and profitability. By gaining a comprehensive understanding of the local market, we can make more informed investment decisions.

One particular region that has been receiving significant attention from real estate investors is the Sunbelt states, which include the southern and southwestern parts of the United States, such as Florida, Texas, Arizona, and Georgia.

When evaluating a property in the Sunbelt states, I usually examine a range of factors that can impact its value and profitability. For example, I may look at population growth rates, income levels, job growth, and unemployment rates, as these factors can all influence the demand for rental housing in the area.

One trend that has been driving the demand for multifamily properties in the Sunbelt states is the influx of retirees, millennials, and migrants after Covid-19. Many retirees are looking to downsize and move to warmer climates, while millennials and others are seeking affordable housing options and job opportunities. These demographic trends have led to increased demand for rental housing in the region, which has resulted in higher occupancy rates and rental rates.

In addition to supply and demand dynamics, we also examine the regulatory and tax environment in the areas of interest. For example, some states offer tax incentives or other benefits for real estate investors, while others have more stringent regulations that can impact the value of a property. By evaluating these factors, we can gain insight into the risks and opportunities associated with investing in a particular property.

3. Risk assessment:

Risk analysis is a critical component of multifamily underwriting, as it involves identifying and evaluating potential risks that could impact the property's investment potential. By conducting a thorough risk analysis, we can develop strategies to mitigate these risks and maximize the property's value.

One area of risk that we will examine is market risk. Market risk refers to the potential for changes in the local real estate market to impact the property's value and profitability. This can include changes in demand for rental housing, shifts in demographic trends, and economic downturns. By analyzing market data and economic indicators, we can identify market risks and develop strategies to mitigate these risks, such as adjusting rents or reducing expenses.

Another area of risk that we will evaluate is credit risk. Credit risk pertains to the possibility of tenants failing to pay their rent, which can negatively affect the property's cash flow and profitability. Our team assesses the credit history and financial standing of potential tenants to gauge their capability to pay rent on time. To mitigate the credit risk, we establish special procedures which go beyond conducting background checks and requiring security deposits.

Physical risk is another area of concern in multifamily underwriting. Physical risk refers to the potential for damage to the property or liability claims due to accidents or other incidents. We examine the property's condition and maintenance history to identify potential physical risks and develop strategies to mitigate them, such as implementing regular maintenance and inspection procedures.

Operational risk is another area of risk that we evaluate. In real estate, operational risk pertains to the possibility that internal problems like mismanagement or fraudulent activities may affect the property's worth and earnings. To address such risks, we have robust operational procedures and use our in-house property management service. This involves imposing rigorous financial controls and supervision measures.

Legal and regulatory risks are also important to consider in multifamily underwriting. Legal and regulatory risks can include zoning and land use regulations, environmental concerns, and compliance with fair housing laws. We examine the property's compliance history and regulatory environment to identify potential legal and regulatory risks and develop strategies to mitigate them, such as working with legal and regulatory experts to ensure compliance.

Risk analysis is a critical component of multifamily underwriting, and we must carefully evaluate a range of factors that can impact the property's value and profitability.

To sum it up, multifamily underwriting is a complex process that involves careful analysis and evaluation of factors such as cash flow, market trends, and risk assessment. However, by understanding and considering these factors, we can make informed investment decisions that maximize the property's investment potential and generate the highest possible return on investment. Whether you are an experienced investor or just starting out, it is important to evaluate each investment opportunity carefully and develop strategies to mitigate risks and maximize investment potential. With the right knowledge, resources, and team, success in the multifamily real estate investing world is within reach.

Are you ready now for my Secret to Success? It's not some magical formula or hidden hack, it's something that I live and breathe every single day. I call it "BE there before you be there". Pardon, if my non-native speaking English made it awkward! Now, let me break it down for you. The first "BE" is all about your emotional state and mindset. Are you a "half-empty" or "half-full" kind of person? Do you believe in the power of attraction? Are you constantly striving to learn and take massive action? These are all crucial components to being successful in life. You need to embody that positive energy, to live and breathe it, before you can achieve financial abundance. Trust me, it works.

As you become more successful, it's even more important to continue striving toward being a better person. This means becoming a better human being and leader, by being kinder, more compassionate, more forgiving, more focused, more confident, more aware, more knowledgeable, more authentic, more driven, more inner-peaceful, and more responsible. It is also important to define your company's purpose and ensure that all actions align with it. For example, my company's purpose is to impact the lives of 1,000,000 people with housing and investment choices. So go ahead, make yours even greater. Get that positive energy flowing and watch the abundance roll in!

Remember, the first step towards success is to become the person you want to BE and embody that mindset every day.

I want to take a moment now to be vulnerable and share my weaknesses with you. I hope you can see me as a fellow human being, with all my flaws and imperfections. I must confess, I still speak English with an accent, so if you are a native English speaker, you have an advantage over me. Moreover, I don't have the physical strength that most construction company owners possess, which puts me at a disadvantage compared to male entrepreneurs. Unlike some of you, I don't have the luxury of support from my family in this country. I had to start from scratch, all by myself. To add to that, I didn't know anything about credit scores or credit history when I began my journey in New Jersey. I am not perfect, and I don't have it all together, but I am determined to make the best of what I have and hope to inspire others to do the same.

I didn't have a phone, a car, or a computer (and believe it or not - even the ability to print out my resume!) - while others did. In addition, like every other human being, I faced a ton of other disadvantages. However, if there is only one thing you take away from my chapter, let it be this - believe in yourself and confidently tell yourself that if someone like Anastasia Makarska, who succeeded without ever having an Instagram account or ever using an ATM machine could *succeed*, then **you** can *succeed* too!

Come join my team and let us succeed together! I feel incredibly fortunate to have a team of talented individuals who are truly exceptional in their work. Simply follow the link below and select "Introduce yourself". I'd love to get to know you better and learn more about your skills and experience. You could bring a great deal of value to one of my teams, and I'm excited to help you grow!

Anastasia Makarska

Anastasia is an extraordinary individual who has made remarkable contributions across various fields. Hailing from Ukraine, she migrated to the United States to pursue higher education, where she embarked on a PhD in Physics program at the prestigious Georgia Institute of Technology in Atlanta, Georgia. Later, she graduated from Eastern Virginia Medical School in Norfolk, Virginia, where she gained extensive experience in surgery and intraoperative neurophysiology over a decade.

In addition to her impressive academic and professional background, Anastasia has established two highly successful companies: Zen-Build.com, a construction firm, and Pinnacle Home Realty, a real estate brokerage and property management firm licensed in multiple states. She also co-founded Eight Three Capital (83cap. com), a real estate investment company that empowers investors to achieve their goals. Through these ventures, Anastasia has made significant contributions to the fields of construction, property management, and real estate investment.

Anastasia is a passionate advocate for giving back to the community and is a sustainable patron of the Carnegie Library of Pittsburgh, providing valuable educational resources to the public. She is a prolific author with several upcoming books that will delve into topics such as assisted living for aging parents and commercial real estate underwriting.

When she is not pursuing her professional pursuits, Anastasia loves engaging in creative hobbies such as playing the piano, writing songs, and painting on canvas. Her multifaceted achievements reflect her unwavering dedication to excellence and her great commitment to creating a positive impact in various areas of society. Anastasia's exceptional accomplishments and contributions serve as an inspiration to others seeking to make a difference.

Anastasia can be reach at:
www.83cap.com
https://linktr.ee/Anastasia.Makarska

Chapter 16

THE MOMENT THAT CHANGED EVERYTHING

Maria Marks

There I was less than a week after the best day of my life, my wedding day, when I got the call that my father-in-law was in the hospital. My husband and I got in the car and started to drive. Thankfully we lived close to the hospital but it felt like the ride was never ending. I couldn't find the words to console my husband so we sat in silence. When we got there we were put in this tiny room. As someone who had worked in a hospital, I knew what the tiny room meant. It was where hospital staff would put the family members of the patient that they needed to share private updates with. I had never been on this side of the hospital, waiting to hear updates and not knowing what was going on. But it was there that we were told he had suffered a fatal brain aneurysm. You know that feeling you get when you are at the top of a roller coaster and your stomach drops? That's how I felt except it was ten times worse. At that moment I was at a loss for words, and if you know me that's shocking! I had never been through this. I haven't lost a parent and when my grandpa passed it wasn't a surprise. This came out of nowhere, like my life had been flipped upside down.

I never thought that those vows that I said – "for better or for worse, in sickness and in health" – would come into play this early in my marriage. I went from a wedding to a funeral in six days. I was supposed to be on my honeymoon, but instead, I was planning a funeral.

While mourning my father-in-law's passing, I was just trying to keep it together. There really wasn't time for me to process what was going on. I was so busy trying to help everyone around me that the only time I could really think and process what was going on was at night. In the silence of the night no one needed my help. There wasn't anyone or anything that could distract me. It was just me and my thoughts and that is where the anxiety started.

I would lay awake with all these questions like, what if this happens to me? What if I lose my brand-new husband? What if I get sick? Do we have enough money to pay for hospital bills? I am just a nurse. What if I can't support my family, my children? I don't even have children! The thoughts of all these what-if questions kept spiraling in my head, and I couldn't stop them.

Before all of this happened I worked in a hospital, and I loved what I did. I have a bachelor's degree in nursing, and at the time, I was studying to become a registered nurse. Working with my patients in the hospital fueled me. I felt like I was making a difference in my patients' lives. All the hours I was putting in was not only how I made money but it gave me a sense of purpose. I thought this was my dream job and that nothing would ever fill my cup as much as being a nurse. But I was still thinking about money and my future. It didn't matter how much I did for others because I wasn't helping myself. The love and passion I had for my job couldn't help me save enough money for my future. I couldn't get ahead and I could stop the questions swirling through my thoughts. I either worked all the time and was never home or was home and never made money at work. I couldn't have it all.

I don't tell you this because I want you to feel sorry for me or worry about me. I tell you this because I hope you can relate. Time with family versus making money is a hard choice to make and when my father-in-law passed it became more prevalent that what I was doing wasn't working.

We all have that moment in our lives that hits us like a ton of bricks, that moment where we either do a 180-degree turn to make a change, or we wallow in self-pity and never move forward. Believe me, I really wanted to wallow and complain that nothing ever goes my way. But I knew that wasn't going to help me or stop the anxiety around my future. I had to take a leap of faith and get out of the rut I was in. I had to make a change!

Knowing and doing are two separate things. I knew I needed to change my path but I wasn't sure how. That is when my husband introduced me to multi-family real estate investing. He had been researching it for years but never acted on it. I was so confused about the concept. I couldn't wrap my head around it. When I lived in an apartment I never thought about who I was paying rent to, I just paid it. Honestly, I had no idea what multi-family real estate was. I thought it had something to do with selling houses or being a Real Estate broker. It was something so foreign to me. I thought everyone was on the same life path. I thought I needed to go to school to get into a good college. I thought I needed to do well in college to get a good job which would lead to meeting the love of my life and having kids. When all of that was done and I had made money I would invest in the stock market! Clearly I was wrong and that life wasn't that easy but the point was that I didn't think there were other ways to invest. Multi-family real estate is not widely talked about so obviously, I never considered it as an option. There was one video that we watched by our now mentor that really sold me on the idea of investing. The topic was mindset, a term that was not in my vocabulary at the time. She defined it as "the established set of attitudes held by someone." She explained that we could have a negative or a positive mindset, but if we wanted to change the world, we needed to change our mindset! It was like a lightbulb went off in my brain and there were choirs of angels singing Hallelujah. Everything clicked; all the dots were connected. I started making lists and setting my plan to change the path I was on and all of that led to 3 steps.

1. Change my mindset
2. Invest for myself
3. Multiply it!

The first step was changing my mindset. I started listening to podcasts, watching youtube videos and reading books from leaders in the multi-family space. The common thread that all these resources had was unlearning what was already known. I had to unlearn what I had been taught my whole life so I could open my mind to new concepts. My husband and I joined multi-family masterminds so we would not only be surrounded by like minded people but also learn the foundations of multi-family real estate.

The next step was to invest. I couldn't help people if I couldn't first help myself. We invested $10,000. Now, that might not seem like a lot to you, but it was everything we could invest at the time. We had invested a lot of time and money in our education. Investing in ourselves first was great because we needed the foundation, but it was all that we had, and to me, it felt like one million dollars! Our first investment was the hardest by far because it was my hard-earned money. It didn't matter the amount of money I invested; it was hard because it was something different, something that not everyone was doing. We were one small step closer to financial freedom!

The final step was to multiply – multiply what I was doing and help others invest alongside me.

We then joined our first syndication team and became partners in a 30-unit property in North Carolina. We raised money from a few investors. Using the education and the new community we were in, we were able to help three people invest in their future. Those three people brought so much joy to my life. It was like I was back in the hospital. I felt that joy again, the joy that I never thought was possible after I left my job in healthcare. At that moment, I looked at my husband and told him I wasn't stopping there. I wanted to set a goal for us, a goal that would help keep us on the track we were on to help more people. I told myself that I wanted to help 1,000 families create generational wealth through passive income – money that would help generations to come. That was the impact I decided to make and the mindset I wanted to live with, and that's the mindset that would keep me going!

It has been two years since I got that call that I needed to go to the hospital for my father-in-law, two years since I took my life into my own hands. I am a firm believer in everything happening for a reason. There was a reason I was studying to be a nurse. I needed to learn how to build trust and rapport with my patients. I had to learn how to find joy in helping people. Our past experiences help us in the present. I just needed to change my mindset. It wasn't easy, and it took more work than I could have imagined, but I wouldn't have it any other way. I changed my direction and changed my future. That moment in the hospital was not a good one. But I couldn't think of a better way to honor my late father-in-law. Since then we've invested in more properties. We became general partners on more deals and started to help even more families know and understand that they didn't have to choose between time with their family and making more money.

Jane Goodall said, "You cannot get through a single day without having an impact on the world around you. What you do makes a difference, and you must decide what kind of difference you want to make."

What I am doing is making a difference, and the type of difference I want to make is to help people be confident that financial freedom is possible!

What kind of impact will you have on the world around you?

What difference will you make?

What moment in life impacts you enough to make that change?

My goal to help 1,000 families create generational wealth through passive income is ongoing. Want to know how far I am in my journey? Well, that's for the next chapter!

Maria Marks

Maria Marks has her Bachelors of Science in Health Sciences from Purdue University and a second Bachelors of Science in Nursing from IUPUI. Her time in the hospital was spent in the Cardiac unit, Medical Surgical unit and Operating room. It was there where she found a passion for helping people.

She left the healthcare industry to create generational wealth for her family. She and her husband invested in themselves first by joining the masterminds of Grant Cardone, Brad Sumrok and Hunter Thompson. After joining and learning from those mentors it has been her goal to help 1000 families create generational wealth through passive income.

Maria hosts a podcast called Apartment Wealth to help educate women on how to become a confident investor.

She also co-founded Massive Capital Girls Society. A group for women with the mission to grow personally, professionally and spiritually.

She is a general partner in 700+ units and a limited partner in 2,500+ units.

Connect with Maria! At the website below you will find all the ways to get in touch with Maria!

Linkwithmaria.com

Chapter 17

THE BEST TIME IS ALWAYS NOW!
Power by the Numbers and Beautification for ROI
(Return on Investment)

Barbara Heil-Sonneck

There are several reasons why many more women should consider real estate investing. One of the most pressing issues is the fact that the average American's outlook on one's later years in life is rather bleak; women especially don't seem to have enough saved to get older without having to worry. That's where real estate investing comes in: Just owning one or two little rental houses can already make a difference. Unfortunately, many women, though interested, are afraid to explore this path.

Today only 31.6% of all real estate investors are women, with an average age of 48. The numbers have grown little since 2007, when we invited successful woman real-estate investors to tell their stories to inspire others in the book *The Venus Approach to Real Estate Investing.*

Real Estate Anxiety – Closing the Women's Wealth Gap (McKinsey Study)

Women in the United States own significantly less than men— in liquid savings, retirement savings, home equity, etc. The wealth gap is the product of unfortunate factors beyond the gender pay gap and the COVID crisis that affected women adversely. No surprise that, by retirement, men have thrice the total assets women do.

Key findings
- 67% of women invest outside of retirement plans as of 2021, up from 44% in 2018.
- Women are opening brokerage and retirement accounts at younger ages. Women who are currently ages 18 to 35 first opened a brokerage account at the average age of 21, compared to those aged 30 or older who opened at the average age of 36.
- Women get better investment returns than men, with studies finding differences of 0.4% to nearly 1%.
- Women aren't as confident as men in their investing abilities and demonstrate lower levels of investing knowledge.
- Women's investment account balances lag men's by up to 44% due to the gender pay gap.

Three reasons why women invest less than men:
1. Supposed lack of knowledge about investment products
2. Fear of making mistakes
3. Little interest in financial matters

But that doesn't mean that women aren't any good at saving or investing. In fact, women save more of their money than men; they just have less of it. Women who invest consistently outperform their male counterparts (by 40 basis points on average).

The good news is that more and more women are investing their money. Fidelity reports that about two-thirds of women now invest outside of their retirement plans, and women are starting to invest at younger ages as well.

There's still plenty of work to be done. The gender pay gap limits how much women can save and invest compared to men. Women also lag men in investing knowledge, even though they do better from a performance standpoint. However, overall, there's plenty of positive data on women and investing. If the current trends continue, women could make the gender investing gap a thing of the past.

They can, I can, and you can, too!

My real estate journey started in 2001 with a simple yes. A friend asked me if I would be interested in investing in single-family properties, and the journey began. We joined a local Real Estate Investment Association and attended weekly meetings and seminars to get a solid basic education. It took us nine months and looking at tons of homes before we made our first offer, and after a couple of lost deals, we found our first brick ranch. It was a slightly distressed property in a nice enough neighborhood. Trust me, we made plenty of mistakes during this journey – from hiring the cheapest workers to paying too much upfront, experiencing contractor no-shows, and putting in lots of manual, hands-on labor. We found ourselves installing laminate flooring, finishing some sheetrock, painting, redoing hardware, and so on....

We learned a lot, such as what to do and not to do, finished the rehab, rented it for a year, and sold it with a total of a net $30K profit, not counting our hands-on work and time.

Our real estate quest continued. After the first experience, we knew it was important to have a good crew of contractors, which is key for every successful remodel. We identified our buy box and locations. A place where we and our renters felt safe was always important. The strategy was twofold: Buy short-term finance, rehab, and refinance after rehab for longer holds/rentals, or fix and flip with short-term renovation loans.

When we started our journey, we could not find a lot of woman educators in the real estate investment field. Down the road, we aligned and partnered with amazing women in real estate. After telling and sharing our stories, with a goal to educate and inspire as many women as we can, we decided, in 2007, that writing a book was the next best step.

Destiny or pure luck? I met Linda and Millard Fuller in 2007, and I quickly joined them in their quest to make this world a better place for people in desperate need of homes. I felt very blessed to have crossed paths with such a wonderful couple whose inspiration touches so many people in America and around the world. Words can hardly describe how honored I was when Linda Fuller agreed to write the foreword to our first book, *The Venus Approach to Real Estate Investing* (Linda C. Fuller, Co-Founder of Habitat for Humanity International and The Fuller Center for Housing).

Looking back, it was not the first time opportunity opened doors. The difference was, this time, I was asking for it, grabbing it, and running with it.

Opportunity # 1: Meeting Michael Dell: I was interviewing for a position, and he was visiting the German headquarters when I was there. I asked, and it happened.

Opportunity #2: During my Sales career at IBM, I received a

high-performance award and could choose a special bonus/gift or a 10-minute group meeting with the CEO. I chose the meeting and met my next boss.

#3 Foreign Assignment: Climbing the corporate ladder almost always requires working abroad for a while. Where others hesitated, I jumped. I had one week to decide to leave my home country for a new start in the US, and I took it.

Marketable, Measurable Results: Increasing the perceived value of any property – Design2Sell HOME STAGING & Interiors

Outside of the hunt for finding deals, I discovered my love for "beautification on a budget" design features and home staging for sale, but also for rentals. After years of corporate, I was yearning for a creative, more hands-on approach. The idea of Design2Sell was born in the fall of 2006, and the new company was founded shortly after.

Sixteen years later, this passion project is a thriving Staging Company serving the Metro Atlanta Market. We developed a proven system that will result in measurable and marketable results and the highest ROI (Return on Investment) for our clients. We have been called the "secret weapon" and "the closer" on many deals. Our team has won top industry awards year after year. I am so proud of how our team is running the operation and impacting lives, with minimal operational involvement from my side at this point.

To sell your investment faster, you must sell more than just numbers; you must sell a lifestyle and experience. Let's look at the numbers: (Source - Home Staging Institute)

Min of 50% - reduced time on the market of staged versus un-
staged properties.

1 to 10% - how much home staging increases a property's selling
price.

90% of people are not able to visualize 3D space. "What you see
is what you get" staging has an impact on the perceived
value of any property.

4.5sec – the time it takes to form a first opinion on either a
person or a space. Online it can be a millisecond for a
quick swipe to the next opportunity.

As business owners, we are always on the hunt for advancing
services and cashflow opportunities. Always growing, adjusting,
listening to what the market needs and wants, staying on trend, and
looking for amazing talent are constant tasks.

**Diversification and Increasing Cash Flow: Short Term Rentals –
Finding your Niche**

The travel business is undergoing a significant shift. Large hotels
and resorts are no longer the industry leaders in hospitality. Property
owners and landlords are now seeing a growing market share in terms
of hosting guests and travelers from around the world due to popular
home-sharing platforms like Airbnb.

Diversification is key, and short-term rentals was the next best
thing supporting the 2022 goal: a 2x cashflow increase and owning real
estate for future appreciation. Through a new partnership, Timeless
Destinations, a deep niche "ultra-dog-friendly" concept was born.
My business partner in this venture is a dog lover and an amazing

property manager. Our buy box is high-demand tourism or weekend getaway markets – large land and small home.

We have been structuring the venture as a win-win for both sides. Find a niche and improve upon it!

Portfolio Growth and Sustainably: Multifamily, Warehousing, and Other Commercial Real Estate – Passive and Active Investments

Two years ago, I attended a Grant Cardone event, and that started a big mind shift. I asked myself some serious questions about my business and where I put my attention. Honestly, I wasted too much time on busy work, and even though I made a good income, it failed to substantially move the needle very much in the time vs. money equation. A lot has changed in the last two years!

Mindset is everything, allowing us to outgrow limiting beliefs, reach for the stars, and form a vision so big that the little devil in our ear can't interfere and hold us back. When I started dreaming again, my world changed, and so did the people I was connecting and spending time with: "Where you are going depends on with whom you surround yourself." Being a newbie again, the new kid on the block, meant letting go of comfort and familiarity.

In the last 12 months, I invested in three Limited Partnership deals, converted from a business owner to a shareholder mindset, started a local multifamily networking group, founded my first co-GP and LP deal, co-authored my second book "*Powerful Female Immigrants Volumes 2 and 3*," and am launching the new me. I will continue to actively look for NEW investing opportunities, with a core focus on apartment buildings.

Everything is possible!

Financial experts urge women to invest more and create a solid asset portfolio to secure a comfortable lifestyle during their later years. It still took me 15+ years to finally discover the bigger picture of multifamily.

Through my experiences, I have learned how to find opportunities that give me financial independence and long-term stability.

My vision is to help successful mature women leverage their immense experience and success by harnessing the power of investments and partnerships, so they can move beyond the limitations of entrepreneurship to achieve more passive income while having a massive impact. My mission is to help as many women as I can doing so.

Collaboration and networking are the new currency. Interesting enough, through my coaching, networking, and communication efforts, I started being part of several mastermind groups with startups and new ventures. All of them are thinking big. When you are in a rapidly growing environment with high vibration and positive energy, it is contagious. It's like you are sucked into the fast-streaming flow of opportunities.

My vision down the road is to build a legacy and invest in new businesses and ideas so we can drive change and have a positive impact on our society. Investing in real estate is the vehicle to accomplish that.

The charity of my choice: SAPREA, which works to liberate individuals and society from child sexual abuse and its lasting impacts.

My quote of the year: *"If your actions create a legacy that inspires others to dream more, learn more, and become more, then you are an excellent leader." Dolly Parton*

"Be fearless, inspired, unstoppable for change."

Founder Barbara Heil-Sonneck

Barbara's successful 20 years career in the real estate industry is built on her diverse and rich experiences working internationally in Fortune 500 and small companies and as a serial entrepreneur, savvy real estate investor, and award-winning designer with a passion for travel.

"My vision is to help successful mature women leverage their immense experience and success by harnessing the power of investments and partnerships, so they can move beyond the standard limitations of entrepreneurship or professional careers and create their "rich life."

In 2022 Barbara successfully transitioned her team to run company operations, allowing her to step into a shareholder role at Design2Sell. She is thrilled to be able to take her vast experience and knowledge back into the real estate investing game. A trailblazer in many ways, Barbara is not afraid to be uncomfortable, believing that with discomfort comes growth.

Barbara has held leadership positions in several industry associations. She loves to mastermind, sharing her learning and best practices as a business owner. Her viewpoints on leadership with authenticity, the power of energy alignment, small business growth strategies, and team delegation make her a valuable resource for media and those hosting events, podcasts, and expert panels.

linktr.ee/barbarahs

CHARITY: https://saprea.org/about-us/

CONTACT: https://linktr.ee/barbarahs

Chapter 18

SUPPLEMENTING SUCCESS

Yana Epps

Sometimes pain can be a greater motivator than pleasure. When I sit back and evaluate my decisions, determination, and my "why," it all boils down to one major factor – the fear of not being able to provide for myself and my family. The thought of not being able to put food on the table, keep the lights on, or keep a roof over our heads is terrifying. Having to turn to others for support or go without necessities is absolutely frightening to me. This fear is the reason I have never settled for one source of income; it's why I have a burning desire to do more, earn more, and get as far away from potential poverty as I can. I want to put myself in a position to help everyone I love without thinking twice about it.

The key to financial independence is spending less and making more, right? Financial planners will discuss your retirement goals as if your age is the biggest hurdle, implanting the idea that there's no alternative to working until you're 65. However, the epiphany that changed my focus is the realization that retirement is determined by an amount of money, not an age. This was a fundamental shift for me. I was determined to keep working hard to supplement my income and cut unnecessary spending. I had to stop buying the material things that made me "look like" I had reached my financial goals, things that were keeping me further from them.

Conservative spending has been a skill that I've had to sharpen over time. I grew out of frivolous habits, and now that my understanding of money has grown and matured, I look at a lot of my purchases as a young adult as completely wasteful. I grew to understand that no matter how much I earned, I would never find freedom until I became a better steward of my earnings.

Once I truly understood the difference between income and wealth, I realized that earning a six-figure salary wasn't going to be enough. I would have to make sure my money was being invested in income-producing assets that would create additional streams of income. Imagine making money in your sleep without having to show up to work or do anything. A lightbulb went off.

Before I dive into how I started in real estate, I'd like to share some background and some life experiences that helped shape my beliefs and mindset. I'd like to discuss the early exposure that helped me avoid the hardships a lot of young adults fall victim to.

I grew up in Berkeley, California. Splitting time between the households of my divorced, working-class parents, I was surrounded by the resilience and resourcefulness that defined our lives. Money was not our biggest hardship; I remember having everything I needed and most things I wanted. My parents worked hard to provide a comfortable lifestyle for us. We weren't rich; we weren't poor. They worked around the clock providing for us, which meant they didn't have a lot of time to focus on being actively involved in my upbringing. This left a lot of room for error on my part. As a teenager, I was extremely intellectual but also extremely distracted. While my peers were contemplating career paths, I found myself lost in rebellion and destroying any chance I had to go directly to college. Life had different plans in store for me.

I was eager to grow up, spread my wings, and gain my independence. At the early age of 17, I decided to join the Navy, seeking discipline and structure to channel my untapped potential. This choice would not only shape my professional life but also lay the groundwork for my personal growth. The military taught me resilience, discipline, and the importance of dedication, skills that would help me succeed in almost every aspect of my civilian life to follow.

I was extremely fortunate to land my next two jobs in finance. I learned the proper way to use and build credit, the importance of healthy finances, and the power of leverage and equity. Thanks to this knowledge, I was determined to start building wealth from an incredibly young age. When I was about 19, I was working for a lender. I had a plan to leverage my dad's house to buy an investment property. My dad wasn't familiar with the process of becoming a landlord and managing a rental, but I assured him that I would learn the process and do everything myself.

Long story short, I processed the loan, and with the cash in hand, my father decided to invest with another partner, one who ended up stealing rent payments and allowing the mortgage to default within six months. The bank eventually foreclosed on them and took the property back. His credit was ruined. It was hard not to think to myself, "I told you so!" I often wonder where we'd be today if he had stuck with my plan and started building an empire together over 20 years ago.

Nevertheless, I was determined to own real estate, so I saved aggressively and bought my first home at the age of 25. This was a great accomplishment in my eyes because the prices of homes in California keep ownership out of reach for most. But the celebration was short-lived due to the mortgage meltdown of 2008. I had to short sell that home and start over. I continued to buy, trade up, and build equity through appreciation in this expensive market.

After being at my corporate job for five years, I decided to get a side hustle to speed up the pace of my financial freedom. I figured being a realtor would be perfect for me. I had already proven that I was extremely talented in sales, and I loved real estate, so it felt like the perfect gig. My grandfather was gracious enough to let me list a couple of his investment properties to gain experience.

I'm also thankful to my grandparents and my parents for showing me the importance of hard work and the value of investing. Watching them manage careers while moonlighting as investors is what I attribute my drive to. My mother also found time to run a boutique for over ten years while working a 9-5. I'm certain she's where I get my entrepreneurial spirit from. Inspired by my family's legacy and driven by a hunger for knowledge, I embarked on a journey of self-education in real estate investing.

The absence of a college degree initially haunted me; it was my biggest professional insecurity. Yet, as time passed, it transformed into a source of pride. I've had tons of professional success, and I've been able to teach myself valuable life skills that are more useful than what some learn in college, proving that knowledge and expertise are not confined to formal education. I realized it wasn't too late; I could learn *anything* and be *anything,* and a degree was not going to impact my measure of success.

In 2017, I started my business Ask M.E. Investments. I immersed myself in the world of personal finance, devouring books, attending seminars, listening to podcasts, and networking. I learned different investment strategies and met hundreds of people who were active in the business. While a lot of the information was free and accessible to anyone, I also invested in paid mentorships so I could build a circle of close contacts available to support and guide my journey. Your network is your net worth, after all. I'm thankful for all my advisors. The more I learned, the more I realized how much I had left to learn.

I spent the next few years acting. I focused on wholesaling property to build capital that could be reinvested into apartments. Through trial and error, I was able to close some deals and set some additional savings aside. Eventually, I decided to put my savings to work, so I found a team that I trusted enough to passively invest with on a 244-unit apartment. This was my first time investing in a large real estate transaction. It was one of the largest checks I had ever written. It was scary, encouraging, and liberating all at the same time.

Deciding to spend money on income-producing assets instead of the things that most of my friends were buying took a lot of sacrifice and willpower. I had to embrace a mindset of abundance, detach from material possessions, and recognize the value of building wealth. I had to learn about deferring gratification – making tough decisions today that will pay dividends in the future. Just like that, almost overnight, I had a total realignment of values. I was awakened by the true power and utility of money.

To share these lucrative opportunities with those around me, I decided to focus on syndications, aligning talent, pooling resources, and doing more deals. My specific focus is building meaningful relationships with investors and attracting capital to our projects. Needing help with managing all that this entails, I asked my talented sister, Ria Cotton-Landry, to partner. She, too, has over 20 years of industry experience. Having a partner to share tasks with is vital to scale, and it's even better when you already know and trust them. In 2023 we formed Connected Capital Partners, which specializes in providing passive income streams for busy professionals.

At the time of this writing, we recently completed our first raise, closing on 48 more units in Montgomery, Texas. The next phase of our business will be to launch a customizable fund, expand into other asset classes, giving our investors even more options for diversification. We want to expose as many people as we can to these strategies, especially in the underserved communities where these things aren't taught.

Driven by my own experiences and a desire to break the cycle of generational curses, I became an advocate for financial literacy, striving to empower others to rewrite their own financial stories. Education is the cornerstone of change; I have dedicated myself to evangelizing these principles. I currently host a network of over 7,000 investors and aspiring investors. Through workshops, webinars, and creative content, I try to help others seek financial independence. I love sharing my journey, my successes, and my failures, as well as providing practical tools and invaluable insights to those eager to create a brighter financial future.

I recognize that true transformation requires a holistic approach. I often counsel others on the importance of mindset, self-care, and the cultivation of healthy habits. This includes incorporating exercise, healthy eating, and structure into your routine. A well-balanced life is the way to maximize your success. Mindset will either keep you from everything or give you access to everything.

People often ask how I balance being a mother, a wife, an employee, and an entrepreneur. My response is simple – sacrifice. If I want success, something must give. I sacrifice most of my personal time, keeping just enough to remain sane. There's not much time for TV or other social activities. Unfortunately, most friendships and relationships in my life have been impacted by my commitment to success.

I hope my daughter will one day have a similar story of being inspired by her family. As she enters the workforce, I want her to know she doesn't have to work for 40 years. Whether she has a job, a business, or both, making the right money moves early can change the trajectory of her career, freeing up more years to do the things she enjoys. Leaving her not only with assets but the ability to properly manage her finances is my idea of leaving a legacy.

As I reflect on my journey, I am grateful for the opportunities, the challenges, and the support of those who believed in me. Every setback, every triumph, and every lesson has molded me into the person I am today. I stand proud, knowing that my determination and passion have fueled my success and inspired others to reach for greatness. My journey from a rebellious teenager to a self-taught subject matter expert in real estate investing taught me the power of breaking boundaries. I embraced my unconventional path and found success and fulfillment in my own unique way.

I invite you to join me on this transformative journey. Together, let us break free from the chains of limited thinking, give ourselves the courage to dream big, and create a future where financial freedom is within reach for all.

Yana Epps

My name is Yana Epps, but I've dubbed myself "The Property Princess." Don't worry, bowing is optional! LOL. I am the owner of Ask M.E. Investments and the co-founder of Connected Capital Partners. I have a background in corporate sales and marketing and have been employed for almost twenty years with the same company. Throughout my successful career, I always felt a burning desire to secure my financial future and explore additional ventures beyond a traditional nine-to-five job. As a third-generation investor, my entrepreneurial and wealth-building path had already been somewhat mapped out for me before I realized it.

My story is about how I overcame the troubles of adolescence, found reform in the military, and built my businesses while working a full-time job, all without a formal education. Investing in real estate became my key to financial freedom, allowing me to can spend more time doing the things I love, like being with family, traveling, fishing, golfing, and cooking.

I decided to document my journey in this manner to hopefully be an inspiration to my twenty-one-year-old daughter and women everywhere who may be struggling with some of the same challenges I overcame. I am so excited to share my story alongside these inspirational female superheroes.

Chapter 19

FROM EXHAUSTION TO EMPOWERMENT:
How Investing in Multi-Family Units Changed My Life

Gabrielle Walker

When I was first approached to write this article, both my heart and mind were filled with disbelief. How could someone like me write on a topic such as this and hold the interest of the reader? I am both humbled by and thankful for this opportunity.

My journey began as a little Haitian girl born in the city of Port-Au-Prince. Growing up, I was just like most other little girls. I enjoyed playing with dolls, having tea parties, and making mud pies. With my humble upbringing and less than privileged mindset, I thought owning and investing in real estate was a dream that only rich people could achieve. However, I was taught to want more out of life by my mother. My mother is no longer with us, but I feel her presence every day. She was a remarkable woman who made it possible for me, my siblings, and my father to emigrate to the United States by way of Dorchester, Massachusetts. Coming to America was a life-changing event. My mother worked five long years to get her family to this country so we could have a better life. We were not smuggled in but rather flown here with valid and legal visas with qualifications for residency. This is particularly important because, as the youngest in my family, I felt the heavy burden of making my family's dream come true in the United States.

Fast forward twenty-five years, and my life is quite different. I am a wife, mother, registered nurse, and nurse practitioner. Typically, I worked the third shift as an RN because I did not want my accent to be an issue for the doctors, nurses, and patients. In hindsight, working the third shift turned out to be a blessing; it gave me the flexibility I needed to balance a wife, mother of three young kids, and a healthcare professional.

My transition into real estate began after I had just completed my third overnight twelve-hour shift as an ICU registered nurse. I was on my way home, fighting to stay awake behind the wheel. Most times, I would talk to my father while driving home. However, on this day he was not available, so I drove to a nearby parking lot to take a short nap. My phone began to ring incessantly. It was my brother calling to inform me about the passing of our mother. I was truly devastated. Although I have a family of my own, hearing this news made it hard for me to think. My mother was my guiding light. She influenced, as well as inspired, me to always want more out of life. I can hear her voice asking me, "Are you happy, and is this what you want to do?" The answer to both questions was no. I was not happy, and I was not doing what I wanted to do. However, I had no idea what it was I wanted to do. Four months later, I left my job, still not having a clue. I became a travel nurse and worked at different hospitals around the country during the Covid-19 pandemic. While on assignment in Texas, I was watching TV and saw Grant Cardone as a guest. He talked about creating generational wealth by investing in real estate.

As he was speaking, I could feel my spirit lifting. Could this be what I was looking for?

As Grant Cardone (GC) spoke, my whole outlook on finances changed completely. Conventional financial programs at the time advised that you should open a 401K and save to build wealth by having multiple accounts. GC said this was brainwashing the middle class. He also said that the current tax system was basically unfair because those in the middle class paid more in taxes than the wealthiest one percent. As a person who considered themselves very smart when it came to money this revelation blew me away. I began reading everything I could about multi-family real estate investments. His philosophy espouses buying and investing in multi-family units to improve your financial standing and build generational wealth. Armed with all this new information, I still was not totally convinced that this philosophy on money was truly the best option for me.

Before I go any further, let me tell you my previous beliefs about money and finances. I once followed the philosophy of people who said to pay off all debts and live debt free. They further stated that living debt free is the only way to save money and accumulate wealth. This misinformation was like a drug to me. I read all their books and attended several of their seminars. I had to be there in person and see for myself what was going on. As devoted as I was to them, it was unsettling to hear someone else's point of view about money. Was I wrong for following these people and their theory for creating wealth? This was a hard pill to swallow. I felt that I was misled, and it would be difficult for me to trust anyone else to that same extent. So, I proceeded with caution when I chose to follow GC's teachings. I continued to work as a travel nurse, but I kept up with what was happening with

GC. Whenever he was a guest on any talk show, I would try to watch. I continued to read his books and listen to his podcasts. Despite all this involvement, however, I still felt like something was missing, so I decided to attend one of his seminars in person. I don't mind telling you that I was very nervous and apprehensive about this move. I had been misled before about wealth building, and I did not want to go through that again.

I attended my first conference with GC in Miami, FL, back in 2021. I felt relaxed and at home upon entering the conference room. GC personally greeted the conference attendees. He had a calm manner about him that immediately put me at ease. As the conference proceeded, I became more and more engaged. Feelings of relief and contentment washed over me, and I could not wait until I would be able to take part in my first real estate deal. In the real estate investment game, I am what is known as a passive investor. This means that I don't invest full-time, and I continue to work as an insurance producer and nurse practitioner to support myself.

Let me explain what a passive investor does. A passive investor is one of a group of investors that provides the financing to purchase multi-family units.

The operators of the deal pitch a proposal, and as an investor, you evaluate if the deal is a good fit for you. Through multi-family investing, I truly understand the bible scripture, "A good man leaves an inheritance to his children's children" (Proverbs 13:22). The official duties of a passive investor are providing financial and essential resources for the investment group. The unofficial duties of a passive investor are performing due diligence on deals presented to the group and developing and researching other new avenues of revenue in order to finance new deals.

I can still remember my first deal like it was yesterday. This was a whole new world with new people thinking so much differently and more ambitiously than I had ever experienced. My family and friends were still thinking the same way, so I knew I had to get this right or hear, "I told you so."

Another unspoken duty of a passive investor, which I didn't mention earlier, is to assist the general partner in researching and completing deals that are presented to the group. A general partner is like the unofficial leader of the investment group. My goal is to be a general partner in a deal. I am looking for the right team to be a part of, consisting of ethical people with strong family values. Until then, I will keep researching deals, educating myself on real estate, and associating with like-minded people.

Multi-family investing is a team sport, so networking is an essential component of this practice. Networking is the best way to meet people and put yourself out there. In the real estate investment community, networking also allows you to establish trusted contacts that are important in any investment deal. This journey has been so amazing. The people I have met have become part of my life. They have shaped who I am today, and I will forever be grateful for the privilege of knowing them.

As your deal develops, it is crucial to understand the time frame you are working within. In most deals, it will average around six to eight months before you see your first distribution. Now, every three months, I get paid from my real estate deals. This is what is known as passive income. Take time to study your deals as well as the people you are doing the deals with. Remember to ask questions. Whatever you do, make sure the people you do business with are legitimate.

The question that I am often asked is, "How do I save enough money to start investing in real estate?" Many people don't know that life insurance can be a way to start investing in real estate. As a national insurance producer, I suggest that you start a whole life policy with a death and living benefit. With whole life insurance, part of the policy goes toward your death benefits, and part goes toward living benefits. It's like a savings account that functions in more than one way, and the interest rate is so much higher than what the bank gives you. Once the cash value on the policy builds to a substantial value, you can pull it out and put it toward real estate deals. When you pull that money out from the whole life policy, it's tax-free. This money also produces residual income. The goal is to have money working for you while you sleep. Money rule number one: Pay yourself first and put that money on a whole life insurance policy. Stop using money to support your lifestyle and start using money to create the life of your dreams. Use life insurance as the bank in which you store your money.

In conclusion, make it a habit to study and learn daily, and don't ever grow tired of learning and trying to improve yourself. Try to surround yourself with people who have the same desire for learning and that will motivate you to stay focused on your ultimate goals. How do you find them? Go where they go and be willing to be uncomfortable among them. Attend professional conferences, and your intuition will tell you when you are in the right place. Speak up, look professional, and look people in the eyes. You have what it takes, so always exert confidence.

Don't make excuses; stay busy acting. You are full of life and possibilities. You were created to live a life full of joy, excitement, curiosity, and boldness. Don't let your past dictate who you are; live in the now. Break out of this lack mentality, remember who you are, and unleash who you were meant to be. Difficult financial moments are going to come, but you owe it to yourself to tap into your greatness, even when you don't know what that entails. Cry if you must but keep moving forward. Stay active even when you feel like crying, and people ask you, "Who do you think you are?" You can live your best life now without worries of money and fear of debt.

Gabrielle Walker

Gabrielle Walker is an accomplished professional with a diverse background. As a psychiatric mental health practitioner and national insurance producer for health, life, and Medicare, she has helped countless individuals navigate the complexities of healthcare and insurance.

Born and raised in Port-Au-Prince, Gabrielle moved to Boston, MA, in 1987, where she began her career in nursing. She later earned a bachelor's degree in nursing from the University of Massachusetts at Amherst, followed by a master's degree in nursing from Walden University.

Today, Gabrielle resides in Georgia with her husband and three daughters. When she's not working, she enjoys reading, exercising, gardening, and participating in various outdoor activities.

In addition to her professional pursuits, Gabrielle is also the owner of Pamphile Investments. She has a keen interest in multi-family real estate and is always on the lookout for new investment opportunities. Her entrepreneurial spirit and passion for helping others have been instrumental in her success, both in business and in life.

pamphileinvestments.com

https://www.linkedin.com/in/gabrielle-walker-568427267/

Facebook: Gabrielle L. Walker (iamgabby)

Instagram: iamgabby10x

https://www.inspiredsolutions.com/gabby

gabbywalker@myhst.com

Chapter 20

THE REAL IN REAL ESTATE

Kendra Seck

Think of perfect attendance, above and beyond work ethic and taking on additional unpaid projects during a 9-hour shift where you are only paid for 7.5 hours. Imagine being a first-time wife and mom, age 23, while working for a Fortune 500 company in mental health, managed care. Of course, the companies' policies and procedures were strict, but taking time off work was a simple process. All employees completed a PTO form, scanned the form into an email and sent it to their manager for approval, at least 5 business days before the time off is needed. I submitted a PTO form 14 days before my daughter's 'music recital. My manager did not acknowledge the email up to 1 week later. I resent the same email and added 2nd request to the subject line, still no acknowledgement. I walked over to my manager and verbally asked are you receiving my emails, her reply was no. The second email had a read receipt on it, and not only did she read it, but she also deleted it. One day before the recital and still no reply to my PTO request.

Guess who received their first unauthorized day off work? You guessed it, I took the whole day off work and enjoyed my daughter's recital. The next day I was written up, not verbally warned, but written up and this was the beginning of my real estate pursuit/career. I was determined to be in a career where I could make great money and give myself family flexibility.

I applied to over 20 jobs in the real estate field, only to discover the gentleman, let's call him "Big Al", my personal loan officer, had an opening at his company. Now, Big Al was a junk talker and very comical. I explained to him what happened, and he said, "F em', we would never treat you like that, and did you quit"? I quit the job the same day without notice and without a formal commitment from Big Al. I did send my manager an email, hopefully she received this one, LOL.

I was unaware of the hiring process with Big Al, but I knew I had to take a RISK. Turns out, the hiring process was a group interview with 10 executives and 50 potential applicants. After group interviews, we waited one week for a call back. In all my anxiety, I was selected with a group of 25 total applicants. I began the 6-week training class and once every Friday, we took an exam. When you pass the exam, you remain employed for the next week. With the assistance of my higher power and what little energy remaining, I passed with a total of 14 applicants/employees. My first job in real estate/mortgages was REAL.

To my surprise, I was placed on a team with interest only mortgages and first lien equity lines as the primary book of business. Investors became my life, and I ate, slept and dreamt about the investor mindset. I discovered people living in abundance are not selfish with information. They understand the flow of money and how helping you may lead to helping them. Being from a small country town, this mentality was new to me, but it resonated with such high frequency to my energy.

As the investors came into the office and explained their investment strategies and the reason they wanted these niche loan programs, I instantly understood. I don't know if you remember, but I was buying a personal home when I quit my managed care job! Now, I was able to buy a home with a first lien equity line with an interest only feature. I would have previously purchased my home with a boring 30-yr fixed loan, but I needed to take a RISK. This RISK saved us over $2000 per month. Now, I can save $2000 in a separate account and use it for a down payment on my investment property.

The managed care company I quit sent a letter asking what I wanted to do with my 401k, rollover to a new IRA or cash out. I took the cash out check. One of the investors I closed loans for was a Realtor. She gave me her MLS login and told me to learn how to use it. MLS became my new hobby. I would write contracts at 50% of the asking price and send them to the listing agent. I wrote almost 20 contracts before a listing agent accepted one. I had no idea how to flip a house, but I had to take a RISK.

Upon binding contract, I began to call contractors for estimates. I had no idea; some contractors would give a low-ball estimate to earn your business and then stop the work to ask for more money before completing the job. I encountered four scamming contractors before locating one, just 1, angel general contractor. I paid over 45 thousand dollars more than I should have paid for the renovations. The profit from the project was initially projected to be 80,000. After all my not knowing and learning on the job, I failed my way to 20,000 profits. A 20,000 RISK! I went on to complete 23 home flips in the next 3 years.

This brings me to "The REAL in REAL ESTATE RISK." Less than 1 month after my 23rd flip the 2007- 2008 global market tank occurred. The housing market crash of 2007-2008 was a catastrophic event in the history of the United States housing market. This event led to a severe economic recession impacting millions of fellow citizens. The crash was primarily caused by a combination of RISK, including the high levels of debt, a lack of regulation in the financial sector and the subprime mortgage crisis.

New and seasoned investors can be attracted to the trend of real estate without taking into consideration the risk, mainly due to the high rate of return potential. It is recommended that you conduct thorough research before leaping into any real estate project. Like risk in other investments, you will experience risk in real estate investment that can hinder your generational wealth goals.

Contingent upon numerous factors, your comfortability in risk will vary. For instance, a seasoned investor may be more aggressive, and a new investor may be more conservative. Regardless of the number of real estate transactions you have conducted, age and the ease levels, there are always risk associated when investing in real estate. Here are four primary RISKS when investing in real estate:

Market

Locations

Tenants

Cashflow

There are many variables that affect market conditions such as the state of the economy, interest rates, laws/rules and unprecedented national and international crises. The latest example is the COVID-19 pandemic. With nationwide halts and blockages at the ports, investing was discouraged as the demand initially decreased, then raced to increase price, interest rates and closing cost. Forecasting the market can be difficult, however it is essential to stay up to date on current market shifts. Consequently, keeping track of the market can help prevent being short on liquidity. The availability of access to your equity/assets in real estate can vary based on credit, debt to income ratio, appraised value and location.

Location, location and you guessed it more location is one of the top RISK! The location of real estate within itself is a RISK. For many the attraction to real estate is the location and the surroundings. It is good to scope out a neighborhood during the day and night. The neighborhood atmosphere may drastically adjust based on the time of day. In addition, be knowledgeable about closest necessities such as grocery stores, schools, hospitals, shopping malls, etc. It is not just the present amenities that matter, but future ones as well. Plans for new schools, hospitals, public transportation, and other civic infrastructure can dramatically improve property values in the area. If you are flipping real estate, it's important to see other flips in the area, especially if it is inner city. Suburban you may not see flips in the neighborhood. Homes in cities that have little room for expansion tend to be more valuable than those in cities/areas that have plenty of room.

Tenants are another important RISK. Finding a reliable tenant is key, don't be eager to accept your applicants unless they meet standard criteria. Normally the criteria should be a good previous rental history, a monthly income of two times the rent or more, good credit and any other requirements you may have. Furthermore, vetting your tenants will aid in as few as possible vacancies. It's clear we will have extraordinary situations, for example, a tenant's job loss or workers compensation, but these should be far and few in between when you properly screen your tenants. Also, don't be afraid of government assistance and the stigma surrounding housing choice vouchers, VASH – VA vouchers, etc. During our latest pandemic, millions of tenants were not able to pay rent, but guess who received their monthly rental payments like clockwork, landlords accepting government subsidized and voucher programs. NOTE TO LANDLORDS – STAY OUT OF COURT AS MUCH AS POSSIBLE!!!

Another RISK is cashflow! While cashflow is a huge bonus in real estate it can also be a huge challenge. A lack of cash flow is every property investor's nightmare. You'll be responsible for the principal, interest, insurance, taxes, HOA, maintenance and repairs. The financial industry and mortgage industry recommend six months of reserves per property. If you do not have six months reserves for all properties you own, you are in cashflow deficiency. Every investor will need to calculate their cash flow and expenses to prevent having to file for bankruptcy, negative marks on your credit or your companies' credit, looming foreclosure, using money from one property to sustain another property and many other possible challenges.

TIP:

There's another aspect of real estate RISK that tends to surprise people. Landlord vs Houselord - Let's say you've narrowed your choices to two homes that stand side by side in a great neighborhood. One needs repairs and updates but has a huge land lot. The other is in tip-top shape but sits on a land lot half the size of the fixer-upper. The prices of the two homes are similar. Which do you choose? In most cases, a house in need of repairs is the better investment.

Let's dissect why: your house is a depreciating asset. Real estate says landlords, not houselords. The lot will maintain its value (or likely appreciate) relative to the house. If you bulldozed both houses, the larger lot would sell for more. So, if you can, choose a bigger, better-shaped, or better-situated lot over a nicer house. A less attractive house can always be updated, added to, or replaced altogether, but the lot in most cases won't change.

~May your RISK be wise, and your common sense make sense

~Kendra "Kay" Seck

Kendra Seck

Kendra "Kay" Seck is a multifaceted Real Estate professional with over 20 years' experience. Kendra is Federally licensed by the Nationwide Mortgage Licensing System, and State licensed by The Georgia Department of Banking and Finance, the Florida Office of Finance Regulation, and the North Carolina Commission of Banks as a Mortgage Area Branch Manager. She is licensed by the Georgia Real Estate Commission as a Real Estate Broker. Kendra has been awarded the AIRBNB Superhost designation from AIRBNB sixteen (16) times. She is a Global three (3) time Best Selling Author on Amazon with book "Expert Profiles Volume 4, Conversations with Influencers & Innovators", climbing all the way to Number One, #1, in the Service Industry category, and reaching Number Two #2, in the Financial Services Industry. In addition, retail royalties from the sale of the book go to benefit the Global Autism Project. Kendra was an Area Manager for two Global Billion-Dollar companies, heading up Sales, Operations, Training and Retention. She is also a Commercial Real Estate Syndication passive and active investor.

Mrs. Seck is the Founder and CEO of PsychWeight Foundation, Inc., a non-profit corporation for prevention of veteran homelessness and domestic violence. PsychWeight Foundation utilizes commercial real estate buildings to house homeless veterans, woman in domestic violence situations, housing choice voucher and VASH recipients.

Kendra was born and raised in Metro Charlotte, North Carolina, currently residing in Atlanta, Georgia. Kendra graduated with a Masters Degree in Clinical Mental Health/Psychology from Argosy University. Prior to obtaining her Masters, she graduated from Elizabeth City State University with a Bachelors in Psychology and Criminal Justice.

Outside of working, Kendra enjoys spending time with family, traveling internationally, dancing, singing, cooking and decorating.

Link with me: https://qrcodes.pro/frVUDK

Chapter 21

HARNESSING THE POWER OF DEBT:
A Pathway to Redemption from Failed Partnerships

Donna Hook

A consultant stopped by my cube at work. Little did I know the book he enthusiastically handed me to read, **Rich Dad, Poor Dad** by Robert Kiyosaki, would reignite my passion for real estate and support my goal of financial freedom.

A pivotal lesson from the *Rich Dad* book, which emphasizes financial literacy, is **"The rich invest in assets while the poor work for a living."** The book's asset list included income-producing real estate, something my husband and I had already been drawn to.

Over the years, we'd attended real estate seminars from early gurus Russ Whitney (*Building Wealth*), Robert Allen (*Nothing Down*) and more. Several attempts at purchasing single-family rentals ended in disappointment, as each time, we lost out to higher bidders or more creative financers. Despite these missed opportunities, Kiyosaki's book once again fueled my passion to become a real estate investor.

I cashed in a windfall of stock options and sought advice from a tax strategist. They guided my husband and me to set up self-directed IRAs and LLCs, allowing each of us to invest in real estate.

The strategist introduced us to what we saw as an incredible investment opportunity: an offer from a renowned real estate author and trainer who had connections to Robert Kiyosaki and was even listed on the acknowledgments page of the *Rich Dad, Poor Dad* book. "If this real estate guru could secure properties for Robert Kiyosaki," I thought, "he certainly could do this for us."

We eagerly embarked on this partnership, which included:

- Using our capital to fund the down payment on five single-family homes.
- Guru Partner guaranteed a 15% ROI (return on investment) annually and oversaw full asset management responsibilities, including mortgage payments and fees.
- An investment approach called **lease options**, where tenants have the option to buy the property at a specific price after a specific period.

Through the assistance of an Indiana real estate broker guru partner hired. And who later became our second real estate partner in two additional single-family homes, we paid $35,000 down to secure five properties at $5,000 each. We felt proud to be investors and anticipated our quarterly returns.

Guru Partner returned over $17,000 in the first five years, before the subprime scandal and the subsequent financial crisis of 2008 shattered the real estate market. By mid-2010, the same year the Affordable Care Act, also known as Obamacare, was enacted, Guru Partner struggled to make timely payments.

A surprise call from a Bank of America (BOA) representative demanded payment for our late mortgages. Our first response was,

"What mortgages? We don't have any BOA mortgages." As it turns out, Countrywide, our original mortgage lender, had been absorbed by BOA due to their risky loan practices leading up to the 2008 crisis.

Over the next few months, my 800+ credit score, which I had worked hard to achieve, was slowly being destroyed. I called Guru Partner to share my concerns. Two days later, while at work, he called back and uttered words that would stay in my memory forever. "I'm done!"

My brain couldn't process what he was saying. "Wait! What?"

"The five properties are now yours to manage. Good-bye!" He abruptly hung up the phone.

Left in a sea of disbelief, all I could think about was a call I'd received less than 24 hours earlier. My Florida attorney confirmed a short sale had closed on a piece of land I originally owned with a third partner, who also ran out of money and walked away.

Though I couldn't have predicted a real estate market crash, I realized I'd made a grave error blindly trusting Guru Partner, and his chosen broker, without adequate due diligence or attorney review. As a result of this rookie mistake, only two of the five properties were rentable. There had been no provisions for repairs in Guru Partner's contract, and the remaining three properties fell short of our property manager's standards.

I questioned why I getting deeper and deeper into debt when buying real estate was supposed to be my ticket to financial freedom? What had I learned?

These lessons came to mind:

1. "Guru" status is not a sufficient reason to partner with someone. Complete a thorough due diligence to uncover the potential shortcomings of an investment opportunity and investment partner.

2. Acting with emotion rarely delivers on the financial strategy expected. Instead, use logic and reason when making investments.

3. Seek professional advice and have all contracts reviewed by an attorney.

4. Markets change. Be prepared with a financial reserve or backup credit source for times when things go askew.

5. Monitor investments regularly. Ask tough questions when warning signs arise.

My husband and I had a serious heart-to-heart. For us, there were only two choices: 1) figure it out or 2) unload the properties. After weighing both options, we chose the former.

With a **Home Equity Line of Credit (HELOC)** already in place, a line of credit secured by our home, we were able to carry the rentals and cover repairs for the vacant properties. In addition, I **refinanced** our primary home mortgage, replacing our current loan with a new 30-year fixed with more favorable terms. This saved us $500 a month, a drop in the bucket compared to was needed but a token of relief, nonetheless.

My husband took on the daunting task of repairing the vacant properties. He drove eleven hours west to Indiana and worked tirelessly for five weeks to bring two of the three homes to a rent-ready condition. The third property had extensive water damage from a leak running through the house for an entire year. He filed an insurance claim, and we addressed this property separately.

For the record, Guru Partner's lease option strategy never worked as planned. Neither tenant exercised their option. One moved. The other stayed but faced credit issues and was unable to come up with the needed funds to buy our house.

In hindsight, taking control of these properties, four of which we still own today, served as an important wake-up call. The experience became a catalyst for my professional development in real estate management.

My second wake-up call came from Broker Partner. She was "credentialed" and hand-chosen by Guru Partner. Naively, I believed this meant something. Without seeking legal advice or conducting due diligence, once again, we entered a partnership arrangement. Broker Partner identified two properties: a craftsman-style house for $15,000, which I purchased outright, and a ranch-style home priced at $75,000, which I mortgaged. Broker Partner would take over the operations role, but this time I was smarter and retained controlled the mortgage payments.

In no time, it became apparent that Broker Partner was exactly that, broke. She lacked the financial means needed for repairs and, despite her credentials, also lacked the skills needed to rent our property outside her friends and family group. To make matters worse, she herself, moved into the mortgaged property and blissfully allowed me to pay the mortgage while she lived there rent-free for nearly a year.

By this time, my ostrich days were over, and my head was fully out of the sand. I devised a plan to take control of my investments and remove her from the property.

First, I bought her out of the partnership and released her obligation to both properties.

Next, I informed her she had to move.

Third, in an effort to unload the "water" house, which she previously rented when Guru Partner was in the picture, I offered her an opportunity to buy the property on a **contract for deed**, a contract for the sale of a property which allows a buyer to take possession of a property immediately and pay the purchase price in installments over time, while the seller retains legal title until all payments are made.

She took the bait with one provision: I give her the insurance money. I agreed.

I closely monitored her mortgage payments. About two years in, Broker Partner stopped paying. Contractually, I had legal rights to reclaim the property; however, she refused to leave the house and ignored all emails and phone calls. Broker Partner even called the police when my husband flew to IN to try and reason with her. With no resolution in sight, and a desire to maintain my credit, I was again paying for Broker Partner to live in my house free of charge.

Nearly seven months later, I received a surprise call from my attorney. He said that Broker Partner called him and, after half an hour of complaining, finally acknowledged she was ready to vacate the house and return the "water" property to us. A truly miraculous day!

Our title company was next to deliver shocking news. Broker Partner had illegally signed the contract for deed. Despite a clause clearly stating the "water" property would remain unencumbered, seven liens from five different attorneys were recorded against this property when the deed was executed.

To sell the house, I now needed a clear title, which meant I had to pay off the liens. During my lunch breaks, I called and **negotiated liens** with multiple lawyers. I offered 10% on the amount owed (most took it), and after a few months of focused effort, each lien was successfully paid off, and a clear title was obtained. Excited, I shared this great news with my attorney. He was utterly amazed. He praised my accomplishment and stated he knew of no one else who could have achieved this goal.

The last shock came when we entered the "water" house. We couldn't believe what we saw. The house was completely gutted, except for two small walls in the kitchen. Looking at this sea of studs left behind from Broker Partner, we realized the property required more effort and more money than we had to give it. I hired a realtor and sold the property for a loss. We do, however, still own the two single-family rentals we bought Broker Partner out of.

While I was more than relieved to part ways with Broker Partner, I did learn some valuable lessons, including:

1. "Credentialed" is not a sufficient reason to partner with someone. Understand your partner's strengths and weaknesses and avoid assumptions.

2. Verify your partner's financial stability before entering into agreements.

3. People are inclined to use your inexperience, good nature, and reluctance to speak up against you. Avoid this by taking

your real estate business seriously and communicating openly whenever red flags arise.

4. Verify a buyer's liens before signing a contract.
5. Cut ties with problematic partners as quickly as possible, even if it involves incurring some losses.

By now, you might be thinking my partnership selection is skewed, and I would agree – yet each partner appeared credible and trustworthy at first blush, including my third partner, a Canadian couple "well-connected" in Florida.

Florida was hot, hot, hot in 2006, and I don't mean temperature-wise. Real estate, especially land on the west side, was ripe for buying. I, like many real estate investors, got caught up in the rage.

With Canadian Partner, I agreed to purchase two parcels of land for development.

I paid the down payment, and Canadian Partner, a husband-and-wife team, was to split the mortgage costs with us. As it turns out, they made this same deal with far too many investors, including my sister, and were unable to fulfill their financial obligations. The wife contacted me and confessed they were out of money. Like Guru Partner, they walked away unscathed.

By 2008, the Florida market nosedived. Our Brooksville, FL home lost $180,000 in value. We could no longer afford to keep it, and I attempted another short sale. After two grueling years, the bank replied with a one-line letter stating I was denied. I didn't understand their reasoning, yet I knew financial pressure was mounting.

A discussion with another Florida investor introduced me to the concept of **strategic default**, a decision a borrower makes to deliberately stop paying the mortgage. This notion challenged my long-held principles of financial responsibility, yet, with a nearly maxed-out HELOC, I made the very difficult decision to stop paying the mortgage.

I hired an attorney who uncovered the reason for the bank's curt response. When I converted from a construction loan to a fixed mortgage, I hadn't met the minimum 20% down requirement to prevent **PMI** (private mortgage insurance) from being added to my loan. The PMI company, not the bank, blocked my short sale. They said I had too many other assets and filed a lawsuit against me. Four years later, I lost the case.

Eventually, a **settlement was negotiated**, and I paid the PMI company their due. In November 2019 (four months before Covid-19 started), I received a **Recorded Satisfaction of Judgment.** My case was closed! While totally relieved, I was worn out from the most hellish of all partner backlashes, number three.

Several lessons stood out, including:

1. "Well-connected" is not a sufficient reason to partner with someone. Again, do your due diligence on the people involved.

2. When partnering with someone outside the country, take extra precautions to understand the laws and contractual obligations impacting you.

3. When the news stations and gurus are touting an area as hot, that's a red flag. While there still may be good deals, typically, they're not the ones being pushed your way.

4. Paying for a lawyer is far more expensive when you're solving a problem than when you're working to prevent one. Always hire an attorney upfront.
5. Consider the impact PMI will have on your property.

My new mission became paying down debt. It amazed me how different my breathing felt after the balances on both my HELOC and primary mortgage were zeroed out. I felt a sense of freedom.

Yet, I saw an opportunity to **re-mortgage** our home when interest rates plummeted. However, because I now had a foreclosure on my credit report, my first attempt at a refi was rejected. Thanks to a friend's recommendation, we found a mortgage broker who worked his magic to land us a new 15-year loan with a 2.89% interest rate. Three months later, we refinanced again, at 2.65%.

As part of the initial closing, five "loans" were made. Four were to pay off the mortgages on the remaining IN rental properties from Guru Partner. The fifth covered a piece of land we owned in PA. Currently, the rental properties repay the loans monthly, which covers a significant portion of our mortgage payment. This was my original understanding of financial freedom, as taught in the *Rich Dad* book.

Let your assets pay your expenses.

A newfound interest in Commercial Real Estate (CRE) sparked after watching Grant Cardone on Undercover Billionaire. I've since become a Limited Partner (LP) in Cardone Capital and attended two of his real estate summits, where I met remarkable people.

I'm especially grateful to my learning partners at Legends Equity Group, its founder, Alex Love Li, and the many wonderful people I've met in this community. Through this group I've expanded my CRE education, became a LP in a 30-unit multifamily and, most importantly, have learned the power of trading time for opportunity.

Inspired by knowledge-sharing, my husband and I now host a monthly educational webinar called "**Hook Up with Real Estate**." Our vision is to empower beginner real estate investors with the knowledge and skills necessary to confidently invest in commercial real estate while simultaneously avoiding costly mistakes.

In summary, the most important lessons I've learned about partnerships are:

- Simply having partners with a "guru," "credentialed," or "well-connected" status is meaningless without proper due diligence, including attorney reviews.
- Seek out partners with a "figure it out" mindset, like my husband and best partner. These are the problem solvers.
- Value the support of great partners, like our property manager in IN, who offers us guidance and options when we need it the most.
- When it comes to CRE investing, selecting the correct partners is key. Take time to educate yourself on proper partner selection.

Lastly, our strategic and creative use of debt kept became our pathway to redemption from three failed partnerships. Now, using debt is bringing us one step closer to financial freedom. What about you?

Donna Hook

Confident Communicator Coach

Donna Hook is an international public speaking coach, Distinguished Toastmaster, speaker, and trainer empowering individuals to find their voice and free themselves from the mind-chatter that prevents them from becoming confident communicators and public speakers. Specialties include helping others overcome a fear of public speaking, unleash their story, and speech and interview prep. As a real estate investor, Donna especially enjoys helping her clients in the real estate space.

Follow Donna, the Confident Communicator Coach, on

Facebook:

https://www.facebook.com/confidentcommunicatorcoach

Message her on LinkedIn

https://www.linkedin.com/#confidentcommunicatorcoach

https://www.linkedin.com/in/donnahook

Mention "Women in Real Estate" for a free 15-minute consultation.

Hook Up With Real Estate

Co-host of the "Hook Up with Real Estate" webinar, commercial real estate education for beginning investors, whose mission is to share the knowledge and skills needed to confidently invest in commercial real estate while simultaneously preventing costly mistakes.

Join the "Hook Up with Real Estate" Facebook Group

https://www.facebook.com/groups/hookupwithrealestate

Subscribe on YouTube and watch replays.
https://www.youtube.com/@HookUpwithRealEstate

Work History

30 years of Fortune 100 IT and Leadership experience
Large scale Product and Project Management
Continuous Process Improvement

Chapter 22

THE COST

Sarah Gwiazdowski

Are you willing to pay the cost to invest in real estate?

Nothing is free. If it appears to be free, consider the real cost. Are you willing to pay the *real* price for financial freedom?

The cost beyond numbers

Value isn't normally considered. This isn't a discussion about monetary cost. The medium of exchange is more than money; it is ultimately about time. Time is our most valuable asset, and any cost is equal to time. No matter what other asset you bring to the table, *nobody* can create more time. Time is finite; it is a non-renewable resource, the most precious of all assets. How do we use it wisely?

In American culture, perfectionism is idolized, but is perfection worth the cost? I would say no. I grew up in a humble home, the oldest of five children. We were always taught to do our best. Does that mean you need to be perfect? Reflecting, I believe the answer is no. At the time, however, I bought into the lie that doing your best does mean "being perfect" and paid the cost of doing whatever it took to achieve that. Who gets to define "perfect" for you? I believe only you should get to have the power of defining "perfect" for yourself, but all too often, we give away our power to others, who we let define us and our ideologies.

My story, and how I got into real estate.

My real estate journey began in 2002. It was the end of my freshman year of the University of Albany, and I was at an event, chatting with a girl who was about to graduate. I couldn't believe a senior was talking to me, a mere freshman... How did I deserve this? Sometimes it's those small moments that breathe life into you. That moment was one of those for me. Not only was this senior acknowledging me, but she also saw something in me – something that suggested I was capable of what she had to offer. She offered to refer me as a nanny for the position she was leaving. As the oldest of five kids, I had plenty of experience with childcare. Little did I know the home I was going to interview at for this nanny position would be a mansion. I was treading into new territory, a class of people I knew nothing about.

They loved me, and I became a part-time nanny for a young ten-month-old baby girl. The job was perfect. Over the next few years, it helped me put myself through college, and the family was kind. They were genuine and wealthy; they had all the nice things in life I could only dream of. How had they done it? They were only ten years older than me. What had they done that maybe I could do? Could I possibly have what it took but didn't give myself the credit?

My college years were fleeting, and before I knew it, I was walking down the graduation aisle. What would I do next? Like many college grads, I wasn't quite sure. Unbeknownst to me, I had been interviewing for the next chapter of life at my nannying position. The father I'd been working for was the VP of a real estate development company, and he offered me an interview. At first, I didn't know if it would be a good fit for me. I will never forget that interview. Their angle was to talk me out of taking the position. This interesting approach made me lean in harder. I like a challenge. Tell me not to do something or that I can't do it, and I will try harder to figure it out. I was now determined.

A year in, I wasn't where I dreamed, my draw was negative, and I hadn't brought in the deals. I felt I had failed. All the time invested was for naught. 2007-08 was not a kind time for those new to real estate, and I resigned from the real estate company. It was time to pay off credit card bills. I went into the restaurant business and waited tables and bartended, further developing my network skills. Still, however, that small voice pulled me in and tugged at me to go back into real estate. But I had failed; I wasn't a top-ten real estate agent in my city. What did I have to offer? I only had tenacity and determination. How far would those traits get me?

Another five years went by, and I still had no serious financial growth to show for it. I hadn't achieved financial freedom (whatever that really is). My husband and I followed the Dave Ramsey program to stay out of debt and pay cash for everything. Why weren't the promises of this program delivered? Sure, we had no consumer debt, but other than that, we barely had anything to show for all our hard work. Frustration ensued. Supposedly, this was America, the land of the free and opportunity. What had we been doing wrong?

My dad gave me a book, *Rich Dad, Poor Dad*, but I didn't read it at first. I was now the mom of three little kids, and they needed me, taking up every waking moment. Eventually, however, I was finally able to listen to the audiobook version of *Rich Dad, Poor Dad*. I realized this book had value, and a lightbulb went off. I had been evaluating my costs all wrong. I valued having no debt above all else, but there I was, learning that the cost of my no-debt mindset was keeping us poor.

Wise debt and leverage: that was the answer. It wasn't about saving and paying cash for every darn thing. I needed to embrace debt, an idea that had been ingrained in me to hate, along with leverage, smart management, and focus. Those were the key attributes. It's amazing what the F-word (focus) can accomplish if you stick to it.

Illustrations

One day, I was gardening with my oldest son, who is eight. He is all boy, full of energy and wholly absorbed in anything and everything he does. His version of "the cost of time" is very different from mine (Or so I observed that day). Mason was helping me garden, and we needed to bring down bags of sand for the watermelon batch. My idea of a "good use of time" was to first clear the path, as I was planning and considering how the dolly would need to move back and forth easily. Mason, on the other hand, had a very different way of taking on the task and evaluating its cost. Where I would have carefully removed the large rocks, debris, large beam, and even the fence that was in the way before pulling the dolly full of sand to its destination, Mason chose to bum rush like a linebacker through *everything*. Was his way wrong? Was my methodology right? Instead of telling him to do it "my way" to "save on the cost" of running over things, I chose to observe his method. He got the job done. His way was MUCH faster than mine. Maybe my way would have been cleaner, but would the cost of being "cleaner" have been worthwhile? The cost would have been more time. Did my eight-year-old have more of a pulse on this concept than I did as his 40-year-old mother? I am inclined to think that he did.

The idea of time takes me back to my initial exposure to real estate investing. It was with my dad. He dabbled in real estate investing, but it always seemed to be a burden rather than a blessing. It was always a race against time; there was never enough of it. He had a couple of rental properties, and I am certain the cash flowed well. He always did all the work on them. Maybe this model wasn't bad for a smaller mom-and-pop landlord, but as a young child, I witnessed the cost he paid in time, limiting the ability to scale. Time and time again, I wondered how these properties stayed afloat.

My dad is a brilliant entrepreneur. He has what it takes, but he wore himself down doing the repairs, mending the fences, and going through the court dates and eviction procedures. He used a lot of time to keep his rental properties functioning. I remember my dad being away "at the apartment," taking care of the broken toilets and the evictions. When it came to the bottom dollar, he did get to keep more of his money, but at what expense? His valuable time.

Applications

When the fear of cost grips us, we miss out on the exciting and thrilling adventure of the unknown. The unknown, away from a W-2 job with health insurance, can be scary. For some, this cost is simply too high. For others, the cost of not trying to embrace the unknown landscape of REI and never realizing the possibility of financial freedom is the higher price to pay. Which camp do you fall under?

I am a strong believer that hard work and determination, along with integrity and collaboration, equal good business. A strong businesswoman can and should be empathetic and intellectual. Empathy is a vital quality to have in business that will take you farther than you will ever know until you try it. I am not talking about sympathy and crying over spilled milk. Empathy is the power to put yourself in another person's shoes and see the world, deal, or problem you are trying to solve through their lens. Empathy is vital to understanding your business interactions. Caring enough to understand the "problem" from the other side of the table leads us to reap the most benefits. In my experience, the price of the discomfort it takes to be empathetic far outweighs the cost of being one-sided and stuck in our own ways. Try it next time. See how it goes.

My goal is to encourage you to count the cost. Weigh your options when it comes to investing. It might be right for you, and it might not. It might simply not be the right time, and that is okay too. You have the power to evaluate the cost and the impact it has on your life. If you are interested in investing in real estate and want to reach out to me, please feel free.

Currently, I am looking for joint venture deals and equity partners. Most of my deals are in the multi-family space. Recently, we started exploring self-storage and mobile home parks as well. I love giving the opportunity of a home to people, a place to keep what is valuable to them. If this can be accomplished simultaneously with holding onto an asset with mitigated risk, then why not? If this is something you are interested in being a part of, I'd love to hear from you. Let's connect!

I can be reached:

on IG: investwiththegwiz

by email: gwizprop@gmail.com

Sarah Gwiazdowski

Sarah is an integrity-minded and network-centered businesswoman. She got her real estate license right out of college, nearly two decades ago, and started in the commercial real estate and development space in 2005. She has since transitioned to working more with investors. A real estate investor herself, she enjoys playing the same game with different perspectives and angles.

Sarah is passionate about helping others and loves to make a difference in her community. She is a firm believer that education is the key to success and encourages her clients to invest in themselves and their future through the real estate platform. She especially appreciates the number of tax shelters that the real estate asset class can provide.

She is committed to being a lifelong learner and advocating for women in real estate through constant collaboration with other professionals and a strong networking ethic. Sarah has learned through experience that working together can create greater results for everyone involved. While many in the real estate industry are scared to share knowledge and can have a scarcity mentality, Sarah takes the opposite approach. She takes great pride in setting up clients with a strong team around them to help them be successful in their real estate purchases and beyond.

In her free time, she loves to spend time with her family and garden on her 12-acre property, where she raises chickens. She is an avid learner and is always looking for ways to improve her skills and knowledge. Sarah knows that one of the most important parts about real estate investing is investing in yourself.

Chapter 23

LEVERAGING REAL ESTATE AS A VETERAN AND BUSINESS OWNER

Emily Bullock

It was a warm fall day, and I was feeling pretty on top of the world as a young twenty-something, attending graduate school and signing paperwork to close on my first house. I was proud of myself because I was buying my first property at such a young age and still had my whole life ahead of me. I was in my second year of graduate school to fulfill my dream of becoming a clinical psychologist, and I was also recently married, which was an important rite of passage in my family and religious community at the time. I felt really excited at this time in my life.

I found out quickly that my swift decision to get married was a horrible choice, and I filed for divorce 18 months after saying "I do." We needed to sell the house we had bought together, but the divorce happened amid the 2008 housing crisis.

I found myself in a terrible situation in which my soon-to-be ex-husband and I were upside down on the house and to get away from the marriage and get divorced, I made the decision to essentially walk away from my first property. Losing the money I had put into the house seemed a whole lot better than remaining tied to him through real estate after the divorce was finalized. My family had given me thousands of dollars as a wedding gift to go toward the down payment, and I had worked my butt off in grad school, working at the hospital part-time to be able to afford all our bills. It was incredibly disappointing to have to walk away from that house, but not as disappointing as the embarrassment of making such a hasty choice to get married and having that crumble before me. I guess you live and you learn, right?

I learned so much in that situation, and I am so grateful that it didn't scare me out of buying another property a few years later. I pulled myself out of the despair and embarrassment of the short marriage and divorce and bought my next house as a single woman at the ripe old age of 26 during my second assignment as an Air Force officer in 2010.

I made the decision in graduate school to join the military to continue my clinical psychology training and post-doc and to have a steady income and benefits. One of the big reasons I decided to join the military was to escape that bad marriage and be able to support myself financially. Little did I know that joining the military would be one of the best decisions I would ever make. Being in the military helped me tap into a lot of benefits, one of which is the VA mortgage loan program. As a result, I was able to buy my second property with zero down.

I bought a cute little new-construction townhouse right outside Hill Air Force Base in Utah shortly after my doctoral graduation. The property began increasing in value immediately, and as of the time of this writing, I have had it for thirteen years. I ended up entering another marriage with a man who owned his own townhouse, and when I moved in with my new husband, I decided to keep my townhouse and rent it out for some additional income. We lived in his townhouse for a couple of years until we had our first baby, and then we turned his townhouse into a second rental property. We bought a single-family home in a cute little suburb in Utah to give us room to grow our little family.

I was lucky enough to be able to use my VA entitlement on the single-family home as well, so we were able to get into it with zero down and begin building equity immediately. We lived in that home with our two kids and loved watching them grow. The neighborhood had an equestrian center along with a horse trail and walking path all around its perimeter. We have so many good memories of family walks on the path behind our house with the kids riding their tricycles and scooters as we watched the sunset and fed the horses on those beautiful Utah evenings. Unfortunately, another divorce was in the cards for me, but we sold that property right when the Utah housing market exploded in 2020 and made a pretty penny off the equity we had built over those five years.

I am so grateful that I had held onto my townhouse property by the Air Force Base because I was able to move into it at the beginning of the divorce. Luckily, the divorce coincided with the end of a lease for my tenants at the time. The kids and I lived in that townhouse for about a year until we couldn't take it anymore because it was way too small for the three of us, all our things, and our new puppy, Coconut. Once again, I was able to buy another home with my VA entitlement with zero down during the housing market rise. This home, still my current residence, ended up increasing in value by $150k within the first six months after closing, which still shocks me when I think about it! I knew it was a risk to buy the home when the market had already increased so much, but it was a great risk to take because the market continued climbing after I closed in January 2021.

Backing up to 2013, when my first baby was born, I decided to separate from the military so I could spend more time with her. I was pretty burned out after working my butt off through college and graduate school and then working 60+ hours a week in the military for five and a half years. I decided to start my own business after exiting the military. I "hung my shingle" in 2013 and continued providing psychology services to the military community from my private practice off-base. I rented three different offices over the next eight years and felt sick about basically "throwing away" money on a lease. I set a goal to purchase commercial office space for my company, but it felt overwhelming to think about where I would come up with a down payment for such a high price point. I searched around for office space for a few years, but it was never possible to pull the trigger, as I didn't have that kind of cash available to me.

When the housing market started skyrocketing between 2020 and 2021, I knew the opportunity had arrived to start leveraging the existing real estate I had. I began to learn the important lessons of leveraging real estate and was able to pull equity out of my "golden child" townhouse that I had purchased in 2010. Not only had that property been cash-flowing nearly $1,000/month in rental income for years, but now I could leverage the property to purchase my very own office space! In the middle of 2021, I was able to purchase the commercial office space I had been working out of for the past two years. This occurred at an awesome time, during which I had also decided to begin expanding my private practice and hiring more providers. We needed more office space, and now I could own and operate out of the space I had loved for the last few years.

The office space I purchased was large enough that I could operate my business out of a few of the offices and then rent the rest out to other healthcare business owners. It had always hurt to be throwing money away in rent, so the minute I bought that office space, I felt a sense of pride and excitement that I would be building equity for years to come and creating an investment for the future. I grew up believing that in order to do that, you had to make it big in the stock market. This seemed like a daunting task to me since I was never very educated or interested in learning about that type of investing. However, I began hearing more and more in my twenties and thirties about the wealth you can build in real estate, and now my ambitions of building wealth for my children and grandchildren are focused on building my real estate portfolio, growing my businesses, and leveraging them to buy more real estate to build true passive income.

Over the last few years, in growing my psychology practice, I set my sights on buying a medical business that was for sale by the same couple who sold me the commercial office space. In order to buy the business, I would, *of course,* have to fork out a large chunk of change for the down payment. Where do you think I got the money for the down payment for that business acquisition? Yep, you guessed it… I leveraged my other property!

I was able to leverage my primary residence, the single-family home that I bought in 2021, to come up with the dowan payment for the medical business acquisition, which is now earning me largely passive income that I'll start funneling toward more real estate soon enough!

I'm incredibly grateful I was brave enough to sign on the dotted line in 2008 at the age of 25 and join the military. The military taught me many important lessons, including how to analyze and calculate risk. I have lived my life taking calculated risks. Some decisions I've made have worked out fabulously for me, and some not so fabulously. I've learned so much over the years in the real estate market and have so much more to learn. I've "won some" and "lost some" in the real estate world, and I'm hungry and ready to close more deals.

The residential real estate benefits for the military and veterans are phenomenal. I have been able to buy multiple residences over the years for zero down and never had to pay PMI (property mortgage insurance) due to these benefits. Over the years, in working with military families, I've heard countless stories of military families buying homes at every assignment they've lived at and then renting the properties out when they move to their next assignment, all the while continuing to grow their passive income through real estate rentals. While it can be a nuisance to be a landlord, it has been inexpensive and worth every penny to pay a property manager to lease and manage my rentals.

I have been able to accomplish many more financial moves by leveraging my real estate. I remember learning as a kid that it was always smart to own your own home, but I had no idea the possibilities that owning real estate could open to me and my family.

Dr. Emily Bullock

Real estate investor, mother to two amazing kids, Air Force Veteran, clinical psychologist, owner of two mental health companies, author, and public speaker.

I was raised all over the USA and England and landed in Salt Lake City, Utah in 2009. I have always had a thirst for knowledge and graduated with my doctorate in psychology before my 26th birthday. I was able to work with amazing men and women during my time in the Air Force and had the opportunity to deploy to the Middle East during the draw-down of Iraq. My years as an entrepreneur and real estate investor have taught me so much about myself and my ability to accomplish amazing things. I've had ups and downs in my business, but I am determined and will never give up!

My kids are great sports moving through life with me on business trips, spending time at the office when I have to work, and learning about real estate and entrepreneurship. I'm excited to be teaching my kids how to build businesses and learn about real estate investing at a young age.

Chapter 24

INTRODUCING THE FIERCESIX

Kelli Nguyen-Ha & Mariann Tran

I am Kelli Nguyen-Ha, an accomplished entrepreneur deeply dedicated to the realm of real estate. With over 15 years of unwavering commitment, I have successfully transacted and managed a portfolio exceeding $50 million in Assets Under Management. From identifying lucrative opportunities to skillfully negotiating deals and achieving profitable exits, I am fully involved in every aspect of the real estate process. My fervent passion for diverse property types, combined with my expertise in property analysis, financial modeling, and risk assessment, drives my pursuit of excellence. With resolute determination, I fearlessly navigate the ever-evolving real estate landscape, embracing challenges as stepping stones to success and celebrating each triumph along the way.

I am fortunate to have two remarkable individuals on this journey with me: my sisters, Mariann and Jennifer Tran.

Mariann is a skilled negotiator and expert connector in the real estate world. Her extensive experience as a business owner, particularly in the beauty industry for over a decade, and her background in retail business management have profoundly influenced our approach to real estate investment. We greatly value her insights and strategic mindset.

Jennifer, on the other hand, brings over 30 years of expertise as a successful business owner in the retail space. Her deep understanding of the industry enhances our collective knowledge and strengthens our ability to navigate the intricacies of retail-related real estate investments.

Together, our team is a force to be reckoned with. With Mariann's negotiation skills, Jennifer's retail acumen, and my own dedication to real estate, we approach opportunities with a comprehensive perspective and effective strategies. We collaborate harmoniously, leveraging our collective strengths to achieve outstanding results and overcome challenges.

As a united front, we are excited to continue making a significant impact in the real estate industry. The combined expertise and commitment of our team ensure that we are well-positioned for success, maximizing opportunities and delivering exceptional outcomes.

Family at the Heart of our Endeavors

Bound by unbreakable family ties, the FierceSix is driven to build a billion-dollar company by 2033. Our mission: empowering a million families with financial freedom through passive income from real estate and businesses. Fueled by unwavering determination, we embrace challenges, grow stronger, and redefine what's possible. Our legacy transcends wealth, embodying resilience, tenacity, and infinite potential. With every achievement, we inspire future generations to dream fearlessly. As the FierceSix, we leave an indelible mark on the business world, united by our shared purpose and the profound impact we create. Together, we ignite change and shape a brighter future.

A Journey from Humble Beginnings

From my humble beginnings as a nurse climbing the ladder to become a Director of Nursing, it feels like a lifetime ago. In 2002, I retired from healthcare, driven by a growing dream that had taken root in my heart: entrepreneurship.

Discovering the Potential of Real Estate

From there, I found my footing in the world of real estate investments and developments. I've had my hands in hotel and short-term rental developments across Texas, Arizona, and Georgia. I've dabbled in self-storage and the redevelopment of retail shopping centers in Tennessee, Florida, and Ohio.

An Immigrant's Pursuit of the American Dream

My story is deeply intertwined with the essence of the American Dream—a tale of an immigrant who forged her path in a new world, fueled by an unwavering determination to thrive. It is a story I hold dear, one that I captured in my book, "Immigrant Millionaire: The Story of One Asian Woman Obsessed to Succeed in the Land of Opportunity." This book serves as a heartfelt tribute to my parents and the roots that shaped me. I offer it as a source of inspiration, a reminder to others that while the journey may be arduous, it is never insurmountable. I invite you to experience my passion firsthand by reading it for free at (www.amzn.to/3b5vi74). May it ignite the flames of possibility within you and remind you that dreams, no matter how audacious, can be transformed into reality.

Venture Investments and Fostering New Beginnings

Today, our purpose extends far beyond the realm of property transactions. As the FierceSix sisters, our collective passion lies in making a profound and positive impact on the lives of ordinary people through our expertise in commercial real estate investments across diverse asset classes. Through Lotus Commercial Capital, we are dedicated to empowering investors, brokers, agents, and wholesalers, helping them close their deals by providing vital transactional funds. Witnessing the transformation that unfolds in the lives of these individuals fills us with immense joy and fuels our unwavering commitment to pushing boundaries and finding innovative solutions. We are driven by the profound fulfillment of knowing that we play a part in someone's journey, whether they are entering the world of real estate for the first time or expanding their portfolio. Together, as the FierceSix, we are passionate about nurturing dreams, unlocking potential, and creating a brighter future for all.

Expanding Horizons and Creating Generational Wealth

Our vision transcends conventional real estate investment. While our goal is to acquire and manage over 1,000 doors in the multifamily sector by the end of 2023, our ambitions reach far beyond. Despite our relative newness to this sector, our passion drives us to continuously learn and immerse ourselves in high-profile real estate events and masterminds, including those led by Grant Cardone.

Through a strategic partnership with Sunbelt Equity Group, we deepen our expertise in multifamily investing and syndication.

Syndication: A Game Changer for Investors

Syndication is a transformative force. It empowers us to unite individual investors, enabling them to pool resources and participate in real estate opportunities beyond their individual reach. We passionately guide hardworking individuals to invest wisely, moving their money from stagnant bank accounts to thriving real estate ventures. Witnessing their financial growth and the realization of their dreams fills us with immense joy, knowing we've helped them secure a brighter future through the power of syndication.

Bridging the Gap with Real Estate Brokerage and Giving Back

In our pursuit of growth, we've expanded into marketing agency services and real estate brokerage. As certified real estate brokers in Texas, we passionately offer clients a wealth of knowledge and guidance, empowering them to make informed decisions aligned with their investment goals.

The Power of Learning and Resilience

Passion propelled our real estate journey, driving us to embrace the unknown. We invested in self-education, attended seminars, and networked with experts. Our thirst for knowledge remains unyielding, recognizing that growth is perpetual in this dynamic industry. Learning is the bedrock of our success.

An Unstoppable Force: The FierceSix

We, Kelli Nguyen-Ha and Mariann Tran, are passionate sisters, entrepreneurs, and dreamers. With our family, we are dedicated to changing lives, transforming communities, and leaving a lasting legacy in real estate. Our journey has just begun, and we warmly invite you to join us on this exhilarating mission.

Embracing the Immigrant Advantage

Embrace the challenges of being an immigrant, for they fuel your resilience and determination. Your unique perspective and cultural blend provide a competitive edge. See opportunities others miss, cater to a diverse range of people, and turn obstacles into foundations for success. Being an immigrant is your advantage, not a limitation.

The Creation of Generational Wealth

Creating generational wealth transcends mere financial gain—it entails instilling core values, fostering financial wisdom, and laying the foundation for enduring prosperity. From humble beginnings, Mariann and I have learned the value of each dollar, honing our investment skills to protect and grow our assets. By channeling these lessons into multifamily properties, we've discovered a strategy that offers stable returns and long-term growth, empowering others to forge their own path to lasting wealth. Our passion lies in sharing knowledge and opportunities for generations to come.

Building Legacy

In the face of adversity, every challenge presents an opportunity. Embrace struggles as fuel for growth, visualizing the future you desire. Persistence and patience are key, for success is a journey. Your efforts today pave the way for a legacy of financial freedom, impacting generations.

Beyond FierceSix Inc., our legacy encompasses transformed lives and uplifted communities through our nonprofit work. Remember, reshaping your financial destiny is possible. We stand as proof that with the right mindset, hard work, and a thirst for knowledge, you can rewrite your story. Stay focused, believe in yourself, and invest in personal growth.

Success is not immediate, but transformative. Let our story ignite your inspiration. Together, we can change the narrative, creating a future defined by resilience, perseverance, and enduring triumph. Join us on this extraordinary journey.

Conclusion - A New Era for Women in Real Estate

Dear reader, as we reflect on our journey and the legacy we are building, we can't help but feel an overwhelming sense of pride. Our hearts swell with gratitude for how far we have come and the lives we have impacted. We stand as living proof that the American Dream is alive and within reach, regardless of your origins. We have embraced our immigrant status, transforming it from a perceived limitation into a driving force behind our success.

To our fellow women in real estate, both those already entrenched in this exhilarating industry and those aspiring to join its ranks, we want you to know that your journey is significant and valued. Real estate presents a world of boundless opportunities, capable of propelling you to millionaire status within a remarkably short span of time, if navigated with wisdom. The potential of real estate is supported by statistics, but more importantly, it is substantiated by our personal experiences.

We applaud the individuals who tirelessly strive and grind, carving their own paths in the vast landscape of real estate. Your strength, tenacity, and unwavering courage serve as a perpetual inspiration to us. To those who are contemplating or embarking on this exciting venture, we urge you to take that leap of faith. Acknowledge that the journey may be arduous, but the rewards can be life-altering—not only for you but for generations to come.

Grounded in our practice of Buddhism, we hold immense reverence for gratitude and the immense power of the universe. We are profoundly grateful for our past, for it has presented us with invaluable opportunities to learn, grow, and achieve. Our appreciation extends to each and every one of you, our cherished readers, for accompanying us on this transformative expedition. Our hope is that our collective experiences, struggles, and triumphs serve as a beacon of inspiration, encouragement, and guidance along your own path.

Peering into the future, our spirits are buoyed by hope and anticipation. We firmly believe that the universe harbors an abundance of untapped opportunities, countless challenges awaiting our conquest, and a multitude of victories yearning to be celebrated. We are invigorated by the profound impact that FierceSix Inc. and our nonprofit organization, FierceSix Foundation, will continue to make in the lives of individuals and communities. Our unwavering commitment is to guide one million families toward financial freedom by 2033—a mission that resides deep within our hearts.

As this chapter draws to a close, we impart upon you this reflection: Your past may have shaped you, but it does not define you. The future beckons like a blank canvas, eagerly awaiting the brushstrokes of your dreams and aspirations.

Our legacy, we hope, will be one characterized by resilience, unwavering dedication, and resounding success. However, above all else, we desire to be remembered for the profound impact we have made—for the lives we have touched, the communities we have uplifted, and the flames of hope we have ignited. As we continue writing our own story, we earnestly hope that you find the courage to begin penning your own. Remember, every success story commences with the decision to try.

Our journey has taught us that the universe reciprocates the energy we invest within it. Therefore, let us infuse our endeavors with wholehearted passion, as we collectively forge a future that shines brighter for all. Remember, we rise by lifting others, and together, we can soar to unimaginable heights. Let us persist in breaking barriers, shattering stereotypes, and redefining the role of women in real estate. Here's to you, dear reader, and here's to a future where everyone is afforded the opportunity to thrive.

With heartfelt gratitude and unwavering determination,

Kelli Nguyen-Ha and Mariann Tran

Kelli Nguyen-Ha is a full-time residential & CRE investor for over 15 years. She has had $50M+ asset in management both in single-family homes and commercial real estate completed Full Cycle"

This is all in addition to 20+ years as a business owner, operator, and manager.

As a Wall Street Journal & USA Today featured author, Kelli's first book is a love letter to her roots and parents titled: "Immigrant Millionaire: The Story of One Asian Woman Obsessed to Succeed in the Land of Opportunity."

As an investor, Mariann has transacted $2M+ CRE deals and $1M+ land deals.

She's been a business owner in the beauty industry for 10+ years and has 20+ years of experience in retail business management. Mariann's expertise is in networking and connecting with people. Jennifer has been a successful business owner and an operator in the retail space for over 30 years.

Together with their other three sisters as passive partners, FIERCESIX, INC was born and they are on a mission to create a billion-dollar company by 2033 by helping a million families achieve financial freedom through passive income secured by real estates.

Chapter 25

TURNING DREAMS INTO REALITY:
Building a Real Estate Legacy for Generations

Sunit Brar

The morning after I immigrated to America, I glanced out the window of my new bedroom and set my eyes upon a quaint red cottage; looking at its whimsical brick face encircled by the greenest bushes and grass, I felt like I was staring into the pages of a fairy tale. That house—and its verdant, unfenced yard—was my first taste of America.

I left India at the age of 15 with my family of four, driven by the desire for a better future. With the intention of fostering independence and achieving personal accomplishments, my parents took the bold step of relocating us to the United States. Upon our arrival, all we possessed were two suitcases each and a mere $100 in our pockets, but we refused to let what we lacked hinder our determination to work hard and create a prosperous life for ourselves.

Transitioning away from a middle-class position in society posed many challenges, and we quickly discovered the necessity of hard work. During the first few years, my sister and I pursued our studies but also ventured into the workforce, an unfamiliar experience for both of us. Nonetheless, driven by our aspirations for a better life and a secure future, we persevered.

Eventually, we succeeded in achieving our goal of crafting a brighter future for ourselves. Along the way, I was able to obtain my degrees, get married, and start a family. Yet, the memories of our early struggles—managing four people with one car, using yellow pages for pillows, and traveling long distances alone at night—remain deeply ingrained in my consciousness.

As my children grew older, I found myself contemplating both my life in India before immigrating to the US and my experiences after. It struck me that if anything were to happen to my husband and me, our children would not have the same financial resources and familial support we had in India. With that in mind, I resolved to take control of our financial destiny. My interest was soon piqued by families who enjoyed generational wealth in America. I became determined to explore avenues that could set us on a similar path, securing our children's futures.

As I started delving deeper into this, I discovered that it stems from a combination of elements such as astute financial planning, strategic investments, business ownership, real estate ventures, and seizing opportunities for investments. I also realized that merely working and making simple investments would not be enough; we needed to do more to secure our children's futures.

Real estate caught my attention at this time, as it offered the potential for higher returns. Although I found the prospect of real estate investments daunting due to my lack of experience, I understood that taking the plunge was necessary if I wanted to secure my children's future. I had recently gone on two vacations—first in North Carolina, then later in Florida—and rented a beach house both times. Along with forming cherished memories with my family, I learned about the market for short-term rentals and observed the high demand for such properties near the ocean.

Deciding to pursue real estate investments, my spouse and I focused on short-term rentals akin to the beach houses we had enjoyed. After thorough research, I purchased my first short-term rental property in a different state. Initially, managing an out-of-state property posed challenges, but we hired a property manager to assist us. At the outset, the property had a negative cash flow, and bookings were not abundant. However, after approximately five years, it began to break even in terms of cash flow. More importantly, the property appreciated in value, laying the foundation for better returns in the long term.

Buoyed by this positive experience, we made the decision to expand our real estate investments. We acquired another short-term rental property, also located out of state. Although it did not generate positive cash flow, it exhibited an appreciation in value. These short-term investments served as valuable learning experiences, allowing us to dip our toes into the world of real estate. Despite the second short-term rental property having negative cash flow, the appreciation in value contributed to the growth of our real estate portfolio. Working with a different property manager for this second property, as well as being in a different state and different type of vacation area, provided me with a deeper understanding of rental property management. It also highlighted how markets can vary significantly from one state, city, or area to another.

One crucial lesson I gleaned from these first two short-term rentals was the importance of extensive research and thorough analysis. It became clear that research was not to be limited to the property itself but should also encompass the surrounding area, the demand for short-term rentals, local rules and regulations, and any homeowner's association (HOA) requirements. Each of these factors could have a significant impact, positive or negative, on the management and cash flow of the property.

By immersing myself in comprehensive research and analysis, I aimed to make informed decisions and mitigate potential risks associated with real estate investments. Understanding the intricacies of the market and local dynamics became crucial in identifying suitable properties and maximizing their profitability.

After gaining experience with short-term rentals for approximately six years, my desire to explore additional real estate investment opportunities grew. I began researching and contemplating how I could expand my investments. Initially, I investigated venturing into commercial real estate, but the larger apartment complexes required a higher level of investment, which also entailed increased risk. While I was open to taking on some risk, I felt that the level of risk associated with these larger investments was too high for my comfort. Consequently, I shifted my focus to smaller commercial properties, such as small office spaces or retail spaces with one or two tenants.

During the analysis and transaction phases of potential investments, I noticed that many real estate agents seemed more motivated by their own financial gain rather than prioritizing their clients' best interests. Furthermore, some agents demonstrated limited knowledge of contracts. With each transaction I pursued, I took it upon myself to thoroughly read and scrutinize the contracts, questioning the agents when necessary. This experience prompted me to consider obtaining a real estate license to conduct my own transactions. I had already been engaged in contract reading and handling the paperwork side of real estate transactions, so the idea seemed like a natural progression for me.

I embarked on the journey of becoming a real estate agent and expanded my real estate investments to include additional properties. Over time, I acquired a multi-family property with 1-to-4 units and a commercial office building. After reflecting on my experiences with property management companies for my short-term rentals, I decided to make a shift and personally manage my properties instead of relying on a property manager. This decision not only helped me reduce costs but also resonated positively with many tenants. They appreciated having direct communication with the landlord, feeling that their concerns would be heard rather than treated as just another number in the system.

By self-managing my properties, I gained the opportunity to personally interview potential tenants and carefully select individuals who would harmonize with existing tenants in the multifamily property. It also allowed me to ensure diversity within the tenant population. However, self-management comes with its own set of responsibilities. While I enjoy the privilege of handpicking tenants and prioritizing property improvements to enhance the investments, there are also times when I must handle less glamorous tasks, such as fixing pest infestations or leakages, if I cannot immediately arrange for a handyman or another tradesperson.

One aspect I appreciate about self-managing my properties is the ability to prioritize actions that contribute to the growth of my investments. This hands-on approach not only helps build stronger relationships with my tenants but also enables me to closely monitor the operational aspects of my properties. It has been an enlightening experience that has deepened my respect for property managers.

Overall, taking on the role of property manager has given me valuable insights and a heightened appreciation for the complexities involved in property management.

While managing my own properties has been an invaluable learning experience, it has not been without its challenges. The task can be incredibly time-consuming and, at times, overwhelming, particularly when dealing with multiple properties or units. It often feels like there is always something happening with one property/unit or another. Taking a vacation can become tricky, as maintenance issues or other problems may arise and require immediate attention.

Another aspect that poses its own set of complexities is rent collection. Although it may seem like a straightforward task, it can become convoluted due to varying rental amounts and different methods of payment employed by tenants. As a landlord, it is crucial to stay on top of rent collection, and if a tenant fails to pay on time or at all, eviction proceedings may become necessary. This emphasizes the importance of thorough tenant screening processes to ensure reliable and responsible tenants.

One key aspect to keep in mind when self-managing properties is the value of having a strong network of property managers or fellow landlords and tradespeople. Collaborating and learning from others in the field can provide valuable insights and support. Additionally, staying informed about the numerous laws and regulations governing the real estate market is essential. As a self-manager, it can be challenging to stay up to date on all the legal requirements. Networking with other landlords or joining trade organizations in property management or real estate can help bridge this knowledge gap.

Understanding the legal implications of property management is crucial. Developing relationships with lawyers who specialize in real estate can provide guidance and ensure compliance with all relevant laws and regulations. It is essential to follow legal protocols not only during tenant screening but also in the treatment of tenants and the maintenance and modification of properties.

While self-managing properties has its complexities and demands, it also offers opportunities for growth and hands-on involvement in the management and development of one's investments.

Having obtained my real estate license prior to managing my own properties full-time, I found certain aspects of property management to be more manageable. Becoming a realtor has provided me with a broader perspective on the real estate market. It enables me not only to educate others about real estate investing but also to assist them in achieving their investment goals. Drawing from my personal experiences, I can offer insights on various topics, such as purchasing or selling rental properties, engaging in 1031 exchanges, evaluating residential single-family homes, weighing the pros and cons of short-term versus long-term rentals, analyzing multifamily 1-to-4-unit properties, considering small office spaces for commercial investments, and navigating the decision between self-management versus hiring a property manager. These are just a few areas in which I can support and guide my clients.

My overarching objective is to leverage my realtor experience to expand my own real estate portfolio, ensuring a legacy for my children and future generations so they can wake up every morning secure in their future. Now that my children are older, I am excited about involving them in the management of my properties and providing them with early exposure to real estate and investment principles.

Furthermore, I am eagerly looking forward to assisting both existing and new clients with their real estate needs, whether it involves purchasing their first home or embarking on their initial or subsequent investments. I derive great satisfaction from helping and educating my clients and sharing the knowledge and wisdom I have acquired through my own experiences. If you are interested in benefiting from my expertise and working together on your real estate goals, I encourage you to reach out to me. Tell me how I can help you with your real estate needs.

Instagram: *https://www.instagram.com/sunitbrarrealtor*
Facebook: *www.facebook.com/sunitbrarrealtor*

Sunit Brar

I'm Sunit Brar, and I've had the privilege of being a realtor for the past four years. I've also been actively involved in real estate investments for the last decade.

Born and raised in India, I started a new chapter in my life after moving to the USA. With a strong educational background, I graduated from the University of Akron with a Bachelor's in Computer Science and later pursued an MBA.

I started my career in the corporate world, where I spent nearly 15 years. However, my entrepreneurial spirit and passion for exploring new opportunities led me to transition into running a small medical office. During this time, I also discovered my fascination for real estate investments.

Being a real estate investor has given me a unique perspective. I've built a strong portfolio of investments, and I understand the nuance in identifying profitable opportunities, conducting thorough due diligence, and managing properties. I'm excited to share my insights to help others leverage the power of real estate.

As a realtor, I've been able to assist numerous clients in buying and selling properties. Through this, I've gained extensive knowledge of market trends and negotiation strategies. I seek to provide unparalleled guidance; whether you are a first-time homebuyer or an experienced investor, I'll help you achieve your real estate goals. Let's work together to turn your dreams into reality.

Reach me at *sunitbrarrealtor.com.*

Chapter 26

THE POWER OF FORMING STRATEGIC RELATIONSHIPS IN REAL ESTATE

Bibi Ofiri

I am seated in front of my pool and reflecting on my journey so far. It has been quite a rocky journey, but also rewarding. Overall, I am grateful for the journey thus far, and I look forward to many more rewarding times.

My Background

I am a single mother of two beautiful girls from Nigeria, I have four amazing siblings. I have a degree in project management technology from the University of Lagos, one of Nigeria's prestigious universities. But getting a degree back in Nigeria was not enough to secure a job, so I decided before graduation that I would become an entrepreneur.

My Earlier Journey

I ventured into a cleaning service business without any support, but then I entered a competition, and I won a grant of 10 million Naira from the Federal Government of Nigeria. That was the push I needed to thrive in my journey as an entrepreneur. A few years later,

I started my own property management company, where I managed about 300 properties, including residential, commercial, and mixed-use facilities. I grew my business and thought it would be the means to my goal, which had always been real estate, but I had no clue God had other plans.

The True Test of Faith

I came to the US to have my baby and then go back to my life; little did I know that I was going to experience a major shift. My parents had been in the US for almost 30 years and had three rental properties and one commercial property. After my dad passed, my mom had no clue how to manage the business, so she sold two of the properties and had only her primary and commercial properties left. With no knowledge of how things were, I came visiting, and I couldn't help because I didn't know how to, coupled with the fact that I was a few weeks away from delivery. One day, I heard the bell ring and noticed the sheriff in front of the door with a letter of foreclosure. My mom fell into depression, and I was left to care for her while trying to figure it all out. Two weeks after I went into labor, I thought I would be in and out, but this gloomy period was about to linger a while.

I had my baby, and I was told she had a 50/50 chance of survival. I found myself between a foreclosure, a depressed mom, and a very sick baby. My world just came crumbling, and it felt like life as I knew it was fast slipping away in weeks. My daughter was transferred to another hospital for intensive care, and I shuttled between the ICU and moving our belongings. I put our belongings together, but then what next? We had nowhere to go. It was a very painful and difficult period for me. We decided to move to our church, pending when we could figure things out. Moving into the church wasn't the most convenient place, as there was no bathroom and no proper insulation against the cold.

A few weeks after we moved to the church, I brought my baby home to our poor living conditions. She was still very fragile, so going back was not an option as she was in no condition to fly a very long distance. I decided to stay to take care of my daughter and my mother. We were broke and homeless, with no light in sight.

The only thing keeping me was hope—the hope that one day this too shall pass. But how?

The Hustle

I picked up several menial jobs to pay bills and cater to my mother and kids. I worked as a security guard for a month. I would stand in a parking lot for 10 hours each day. The heartbreaking thing about this job was that I was never paid by my agent. I took up another security job, then a dishwashing job, and went to more similar jobs to provide for my family. This didn't break me, but it spurred me, even more, to ensure that my long-term vision of building an empire was possible. Although it didn't look like it, my faith was bigger than my fears.

10 months after we lost our home, I went back to school to get a master's degree, believing that it was the only way to achieve my American dream. With my new reality, I picked up more security and dishwashing shifts so I could pay my school bills, and then I picked the night shift so I could have some peace and quiet to read. I did 85% of my classes during my break period, and it was very challenging

because I was still a breastfeeding mom. I was juggling many shifts to cater to my bills and family.

Unfortunately, I lost my major security job because the contract with the company was wrapping up, but I had no clue that was God's way of saying, "Hold on baby, the light is near."

The Shift

I accompanied a friend to pick up his W-2 with the intention of requesting another security job. We got to the office, and I noticed the office had no secretary, I saw this as an opportunity, and I pitched myself to the owner. A brief interview was conducted, I went through the application process, and I resumed the following day as the office secretary.

A few months later, while still working as a secretary, I graduated with a master's in information systems with a degree in cybersecurity. I was no longer content with the level I was at. I decided to have a conversation with my boss to find out if he had ever considered venturing into real estate. Knowing that the current business was fluid, I was confident it would do better if we diversified into real estate. My goal for financial freedom was real estate, but I knew that since I didn't have the money to pull it off on my own, getting into a partnership was a means to achieving my goal.

My RE Journey

"If you don't like where you are, move! You are not a tree."

Whenever I think of my journey, I think of that defining moment when I put everything aside—my degrees and certifications—and chased after a future that seemed bleak, but I was determined to make it regardless.

There were times when thoughts of limitation would cloud my mind—the thought that I could never buy my own house or multiple units because not only did I not have the resources, but I also didn't know how real estate works in the US. With no one to help, I decided I was going to build the bridges I needed to get to the future I envisaged and walk through them. So, the first thing I did was identify my strengths that would make it hard for anyone to say no to partnering with me.

Don't wait for the opportunity, create it....

Strategic Partnership

I had a candid conversation with my former boss and enlightened him about my experience with real estate back in my home country and how I was positive that in a better environment, as we have in the US, it would be more profitable. I was open about my limited understanding of the real estate industry; however, I was ready to acquire the knowledge needed to have great success. He was reluctant but willing to try it out if I acquired the skills needed.

I rolled up my sleeves and got to work. I started taking free classes on YouTube from people with bigger pockets, the likes of Jerry Norton and Ken McElroy. I also took a short course in multifamily on Udemy. Eight months later, armed with new knowledge, I went back to my boss to inform him that I was ready for us to proceed, but he told me that he had lost interest. I was heartbroken yet persistent because I knew this was my only path to financial freedom.

Fortunately, after four months, my boss reached out to me, stating that he was ready to venture into the business because he discovered the tax benefits that came with it. This was how my RE journey started. I considered RE because I am a survivor, and surviving was all I knew. I had to survive for my girls, my mother, and my family, knowing that my current state wasn't going to get me on the path to financial freedom. I had to make it work because everything was at stake.

The first thing I did was create a structure for the business. I was willing to do all the work (sweat capital) and have him bring the funds. We structured the business around an 80/20 sharing formula. I got 20%, and although it was small compared to the work I was putting in, I was all about the opportunity to prove myself. The start of your real estate journey should be more about service than reward. The reward comes because of growth. My goal was to secure a financial partner, gain knowledge, and take the necessary steps toward our financial freedom.

My First Deal

There are different aspects of real estate: Single Families, Vacation Rentals, Fix and Flip, Multifamily, Construction, et cetera. I decided to start my first deal with the level of knowledge I had. *You cannot grow beyond your capacity, so expand your capacity!*

My first real estate deal was a vacation rental and a fix-and-flip. I got two amazing deals at the same time with no practical experience, but then again, I was willing to learn and make it work. I formed relationships that helped me run the vacation rental while watching keenly to learn on the job. Before I got these deals, I subscribed to a fix and flip app to help underwrite fix and flip deals as well as go through the courses. I pulled through my first fix and flip by going through the processes described in the course, and I was willing to make mistakes and learn from them, but fortunately, I did not make any mistakes but learned a valuable lesson: that money is not important to start a real estate business but relationships and community.

Barely a month later, we got another fix and flip and vacation rental in escrow, and we kept improving on it. From these two vacation rentals, we made almost a hundred thousand dollars in income, and for the fix and flip, within 4 months, we made almost a hundred and fifty thousand dollars. This right here was what I needed to keep going; the result was all the reward I needed. My former boss(business partner) was amazed at the results, and he decided to go all in with me.

What is Fix and Flip?

It is simply the process of buying a property below market value and renovating it to increase its value, intending to make a profit after sales. It is typically a short hold with a capital gain.

Why Fix and Flip?

- It is a quick way to make money.
- Fast turn time (you go in and exit fast).
- If done properly, it is very profitable.

Some challenges with Fix and Flip

- It is very transactional; that is, you must keep repeating the process.
- It is a very active business, and if not done right, funds can be lost.

- ~ There could be delays from contractors that can affect your exit strategy and profitability.
- ~ External factors such as the FED and buyers' purchasing power can cause some significant effects.
- ~ It is not an ideal way to own assets and build wealth.
- ~ Please note that this is not an exhaustive list.

My Vacation Rental Business

A vacation rental is a short-term rental of a furnished apartment or house temporarily to tourists or guests.

Some of the benefits of owning a vacation rental include.

- More income.
- Equity appreciation because the property tends to appreciate over time.
- Tax Deduction.
- Disadvantages
- Varying laws and regulations
- It could be seasonal.
- Higher taxes.
- Upkeep and maintenance of the property: This can be time-consuming if you are doing it yourself and expensive if you must outsource.
- It can also be active if managing it yourself.

As the months went by, I began to see multifamily as a better opportunity that could be used as a vehicle to get to my goal of financial freedom.

Watch out for Vol. 2 to learn how I ventured into my multifamily journey with almost 1000 units.

"Buying real estate is not only the best way, the quickest way, the safest way, but the only way to become wealthy." - Marshall Field

Blessing Bibi Ofiri

Blessing Bibi Ofiri is the Chief Operating Officer of Blue Ocean equity LLC and jointly owns 105 units across multiple states including PA, MD, CA, and FL, and is passively invested in close to 600 units in TX and OK and has 243 units under contract.

She holds a master's degree in information systems with a concentration in Cybersecurity and a bachelor's degree in project management technology.

Her background included an asset management resume spanning twelve (12) years. Her specialty also comprises technical analysis, underwriting, and asset management. She oversees all aspects of the business including project leadership, legal and finance, and is fiercely passionate about driving others toward success. She is in the Michael Blank mastermind.

She is a hard- working, and highly motivated entrepreneur who will stop at nothing in getting things done. She is a follower of Christ and believes in God's love for everyone.

She is a mother of two beautiful girls. Her hobbies are listening to the news and singing.

She is also a co-author of one of amazon's bestsellers " Powerful Female Immigrants".

Bibi can be reached at: https://linktr.ee/bibiofiri

Chapter 27

THE POWER OF PERSEVERANCE:
A Woman's Path to Real Estate Success After Missteps

Lisa R. Casanova-Del Moral

One Sunday in July 2021, I was sitting down at my desk in front of my computer, in my home in Puerto Rico. I was participating in the virtual Real Estate Summit of Grant Cardone. I got hooked with the information presented. This blew my mind. The topic was how to invest in multifamily and how they have a new club where you will have access to his material, knowledge, process, and methods to acquire your first deal, additional seminars and be part of a network of investors. All this was for $25,000 and was for a year. I thought this was possible, I love to learn, and will be part of my real estate path that I started two years before. At that moment I took my credit cards in my hand and froze for a moment. I felt like a deer crossing the street in front of a car and got paralyzed looking at the lights of a car. The last years of my life passed in front of my eyes like a movie of all the scams and situations from my past.

Just to give you a little information about me, I was living my mom's example. She completed her bachelor's degree, worked for a private company more than 8 hours daily, got married, had two daughters, completed her master's degree for a better position in the same W2 that she had for years, tried a few multi-level companies and was the head of the household. She hustled all her life, saved her money, did not have any luxury and all that was to have a better situation for her, my sister and me. She retired from her W2 and has enough to be comfortable, but she still worries about the future of her daughters and grandchildren. Just to let you know she is my HERO and I'm blessed to have her as my mom. So, I got married, completed my master's degree, killed myself for my W2, bought a house close to my family and have my 401K.

I work in the healthcare insurance industry. I work more than 10 hours daily, taking a daily commute of one and half to two hours each way every day. Yes, a long commute because I thought that was more important to be close to the family and have a bigger house than the value of my time and energy. My first situation was in 2009, we bought an apartment close to our jobs, but we lost all our investment in that deal. The only good thing about that time was our baby boy. After we abandoned the apartment because of all the construction issues, and damaged our credit, we went back to our hometown, we went back to the long commute and did not have any cash nor credit to buy something else. Lucky us we still have our house because our plan was to sell it and we tried it unsuccessfully.

Our second situation was in 2014, when we decided to rent an apartment. We decided to rent because our credit was bad. We found an apartment, and to be honest it was to good to be true. I contacted the "owner" that lived outside of Puerto Rico. I sent him the equivalent of a month of rent just for him to send us the key to the apartments. You can figure out what happened. Yes, I did not get any more contact with the "owner", and we lost the money. We learn the lesson, but this hurts our ego because we are intelligent people. At least that is what I believe.

The third situation was in 2019. I had a few tense situations in my job, my health and my baby's health during the prior years... I started to wonder if I was working to have a good life or if I was living for my job. I want to clarify that no one puts a gun to my head to work on multiple projects and tasks for long hours. I did it because I felt appreciated in my job and that I owned them all because they gave me the opportunity to keep growing in the company. But sadly, I felt overwhelmed. The problem at that moment was that I didn't know better nor have the courage to do something different about my situation. I worked tirelessly and took all the challenges that my job had for me. I'm fortunate that my bosses gave me the opportunity to keep growing in the same company. But when I did all the math... SOMETHING WAS MISSING!

Then in April 2019, I saw a post on Facebook about a free event on how to start your own business and the public figure on the post was one of Shark Tank main person. I went to the event, and it was full. It was my first event of that kind, but just to let you know the public figure was not in the event. At that moment, I thought that it was because the event was in Puerto Rico, but later I understood that strategy. It was full because the promoters promised to give you the key to success at no charge. Far from true, what they gave us was a few good tips for business, and how through the practice of flippling houses you can make the money that you need to establish your own business. They offered a real estate seminar and a business seminar for a couple of thousands of dollars each. I jumped in both, putting both in my credit card. They gave us more relevant details to move forward in the world of business and in the world of flipping houses but also showed us how to increase the limit of our credit cards. Believe me all of us contacted the banks of our credit cards to increase the credit limits. We believed that was to buy the properties to fix, but it was to buy their educational packages that were offered at the end. I want so much to establish my own business, that I put $25K for one of the flipping houses packages. We formed our company "Real Estate Solutions 4 All", because we want to offer multiple and diverse real estate services.

A few months later the FTC (1) closed that company, and we lost our money again. Before that, I went to a seminar in Las Vegas, Nevada. I saw Grant Cardone for the first time and only for 30 minutes. He talks about the 10X way to reach your goal and we get hooked again.

After this last back step in our misfortunes with real estate, we decided to find our first property to make our first flip. We found it, and it was located 15 minutes from our job place. It was an apartment, and we made an offer that was accepted quickly. Again, without the services of a real estate agent that helps us to look for comparable and help us in the process. Later when we acquired more real estate knowledge, we found that we paid almost $15,000 over a competitive price. But we got the property and started to apply what we learned about flipping. We decided to keep the property for ourselves and took money from our savings to complete the improvements. First mistake when you are doing flippings. Lucky us the selected quote was from a company with high ethical and moral standards. The company also worked in the flipping business and took us under their wings.

When we completed the apartment, we decided to look for the next property. We were scared because to be successful in the flipping world you need to buy, fix, and sell as soon as you can, do your numbers and calculations to take back your investment and have profit. That way you can move to the next property. Well, we did not sell the first property, so we do not have too much money for the next project. We created an alliance with the company that worked in the apartment, and we found our second property, in January 2020. We took from the limited amount of vacation days, the afternoons, and the weekends to buy the needed material for the fixes, to do all the diligence for the utilities, to visit the property and to keep learning.

Do you remember what happened in March 2020? COVID hit us like a ton of bricks. The world stops and our second project too. Puerto Rico had the longest quarantine time and when the people started working from home, the neighbors of the second property did not let us continue with the project. We did not progress in the project for almost six months. The quarantine became less strict, and we completed the project. We received back our total investment and a good profit. We felt over the moon, and we saw a huge potential to keep doing this. But COVID change everything, at least for us. We became part of the 20% of small businesses that fail in the first year of establishment and of the 23% impacted by COVID. (2) At that moment, we thought that we needed to keep working forever for someone else and stop the hustle.

During the quarantine we were from the few that did not lose our jobs and our W2 let us work from home. After a few weeks with limited opportunities to get out of the house, I decided to study virtually to get my Real Estate Agent license, because I want to understand how this works in Puerto Rico and avoid more of my previous mistakes from happening to me or to my family and friends. Also, I kept looking for real estate information and here I was with my credit cards in my hand to pay the annual membership for the Grant Cardone Real Estate Club.

I evaluated all my missteps in real estate and took the decision to move forward. I saw the lights of the cars in the middle of the road, like the deer, and I jumped. I took the decision to not let fear stop me. I was not a victim of my previous failures; I oversaw my destiny and my family's future. Invested to increase my knowledge, skills, to grow my network, to have a mentor to walk the talk about creating wealth through real estate. I decided all this with my heart beating like crazy, with a cloud of doubt over my head and with the fear of losing our money again.

My missteps are my biggest allies in my path to success. Let me give what I learn as advises to you:

- You must invest time and money to learn about the business path that you want to follow.
- The failures are great opportunities to learn what not to do and redefine your strategy.
- Look for a mentor, someone that is successful in what you want to accomplish and is willing to guide you.
- Everyone has the same 24 hours. What is different is what you do with yours.
- You need to be with people that have your same level of craziness and passion to be successful.

Now I'm developing multiple streams of income. I'm working in my W2, a Real Estate Agent in Puerto Rico, a passive investor with 800+ doors (apartments) in Texas and Florida, and a financial consultant. Yes, a financial consultant too, because in this Monopoly's game you need to manage your money and credit. I decided to partner with three amazing companies that have the tools, the people, and the skills to leverage my time and businesses. I will keep hustling and growing my empire of multi services business.

Let's connect and let me know how I can support you in your real estate, business and/or financial adventure.

(1)   FTC: Federal Trade Commission
(2)   106 Business Statistics For 2023 (Current Data and Trends)
       https://www.demandsage.com/business-statistics/

Lisa R. Casanova-Del Moral

My name is Lisa Raquel Casanova Del Moral and I was born in Puerto Rico in 1979. My biggest love is my husband José and my son Ian. Learn, read, share with my family and friends, meet new people, work and have fun are my passions.

My bachelor's degree was in Computers Science & Mathematics and my master's degree was in Open Systems & Database Administrator.

I'm the top leader of the Business Intelligence and Data Management Department, in one of the biggest Healthcare Company in the island. I have more than 20 years of experience.

I'm the president of Real Estate Solutions 4 All, also I'm a real estate agent in PR, power by Exp Realty. I started JW&LC Services to offer finance services. I'm working with two amazing network marketing companies. One gives us the opportunities to make money during our vacations, on cruises or hotel stays. The second one is a Fintech Company that offers multiple financial solutions.

I'm part of the Grant Cardone Real Estate Club, the Business Accelerator Program, and Sumrocker's student since 2021. I invested in 3 deals as LP, with 854 doors.

 Contact me:

https://lisarcasanova.com

https://linktr.ee/LisaCasanova